FIFA
WOMEN'S WORLD CUP CANADA
2015 ™

THE OFFICIAL BOOK

Authors: Catherine Etoe, Jen O'Neill, Natalia Sollohub
Project director: Martin Corteel
Project Art Editor: Luke Griffin
Picture research: Paul Langan
Book designer: Harj Ghundale
Production: Maria Petalidou

Manufactured under licence by Carlton Books Limited

Printed in Spain

FIFA
WOMEN'S
WORLD CUP
CANADA
2015™

THE OFFICIAL BOOK

CANADA
2015
FIFA
WOMEN'S WORLD CUP

OFFICIAL LICENSED
PRODUCT

TM©

CONTENTS

Weighing in at 1.8kg the FIFA Women's World Cup trophy is light enough to be lifted by an individual but it takes a squad of 23 players to win it.

CANADA 2015 FIFA WOMEN'S WORLD CUP TM©

WELCOME TO CANADA

Canada loves its soccer and its women's side has been its most successful team in recent times. Now this stunning country has the opportunity to showcase its passion for the beautiful game to the rest of the footballing world. From coast to coast, playing in six culturally diverse cities and their superb sporting venues, Canada will welcome the 23 other competing nations, their fans and the media, when it hosts 2015's biggest festival of football — the FIFA Women's World Cup.

An aerial view of downtown Vancouver and BC Place, the venue for the final, nestled within Vancouver Harbour.

TO A GREATER GOAL™

For sport, for women and for the host nation, this tournament features the best of the best and the opportunity to carry that positive message and journey forward.

Canada is not only a vast country with astonishing vistas, it is also a proud sporting nation – and football is the country's biggest participation sport. The Canadian Soccer Association celebrated its centenary in 2012, the same year that its women's side won bronze at the London Olympics, reinforcing the Canucks' standing as one of the world's top-ranked teams.

Now it is Canada's turn to welcome the best teams in the world as it hosts the premier FIFA women's football tournament; 128 nations entered, all with ambitions of competing in the finals but only 24 teams have a chance to fulfil the ultimate dream of victory in Vancouver on 5 July.

With home advantage, the hopeful hosts believe that they are genuine contenders to win it for the first time. But Canada won't be the only ones confident of creating waves – many teams have their hungry eyes on the prize, including neighbours USA and European powerhouse

Germany, both two-time winners, as well as current holders Japan and the likes of Sweden and France.

Canada have gone close before, of course – they were semi-finalists in the USA in 2003. They have produced some heroines in the women's game too, such as super-striker Charmaine Hooper, warrior-like Andrea Neil and charismatic midfielder Kara Lang, one of the Canada 2015 Official Ambassadors, her career having been sadly cut short by injury.

Canada's influence in the women's game is not limited to its players either; it has produced pioneering officials like FIFA's former Head of Women's Referee Development, Sonia Denoncourt, and Carol Anne Chenard, the first woman to referee at England's Wembley Stadium.

Having attended the inaugural FIFA U-19 Women's World Championship in 2002 and then the FIFA U-20 World Cup 2007 in record numbers and cheered on their young

representatives at the slickly organized FIFA U-20 Women's World Cup 2014, the nation's citizens are once again being urged to support their team and welcome visitors as they enjoy Canada's natural wonders, culture and hospitality.

Providing the stage for these world-class athletes gives Canadians the opportunity to celebrate not only the prestigious competition itself but also all female players across the globe. The tournament's official slogan "to a greater goal" encapsulates this vision of recognizing and lauding the current generation of footballing greats and inspiring and empowering the next.

"For sport, for women, for Canada: those are three qualities that highlight our ambitions in hosting a successful FIFA Women's World Cup," said Victor Montagliani, Chairman of the National Organizing Committee and President of the Canadian Soccer Association.

For Canada, and for the wider game, overall success would be an explosion in interest, similar to the legacy of the FIFA Women's World Cup in the USA in 1999, matched with the superb quality of play, on-field drama and joyously intense atmospheres experienced in Germany in 2011.

If the "Land of the Maple Leaf" steps up to the plate as expected, then whichever team lifts the trophy on 5 July, Canada and football will also be the winners.

Left: **Canada coach John Herdman holds up the tournament's official slogan and also in many ways its mission statement: To a Greater Goal.**

Right: **The official mascot of the tournament, Shueme the great white owl.**

THE QUALIFYING TRAIL

Before a ball has even been kicked, it is safe to say that this FIFA Women's World Cup will be an exceptional one. That is because it will throw together 24 competing nations for the first time in its history.

Eight of those are debutants, others have been ever-present, and still more will hope that this can be their breakthrough moment on the world stage – as will every player who gets the chance to represent them on the pitches of Canada this summer. All will have worked their socks off to be a part of it – and all know that, whatever happens in the weeks that follow, they have reached the pinnacle of the women's game.

To hit those heights, most will have experienced the agonies and ecstasies of qualification – hard-fought campaigns that raged over six continents and featured 128 teams in a total of 398 matches. The first of those kicked off in April 2013 and the very last was played in December 2014, Ecuador bagging the final spot on offer a mere four days before the eagerly awaited tournament draw in Ottawa.

Fittingly, title-holders Japan were one of the first to book their ticket to Canada

alongside Australia, China PR, Korea Republic and newcomers Thailand, who were in dreamland after holding their nerve against Vietnam on their opponents' home soil to claim the fifth Asian Football Confederation spot.

Seven of Europe's eight entrants were next to reach Canada but it was not a quick journey; the year-long qualification groups kicked off in September 2013. The majority made light work of their rivals, though, with finals debutants Switzerland becoming the first to qualify, in June 2014, with two games to spare. England, France, Germany and Norway went through with a game to go, as did Spain who will now make their finals bow.

Perennial finalists Sweden were made to fight for their place by Scotland, but that rivalry was settled in September 2014 when a lively crowd and their "Camp Sweden" fans cheered the Blagult to victory over the

Scots in Gothenburg. It took play-offs to decide the final coveted European place, four of the best runners-up battling it out home and away, with the Netherlands going on to put their name in the draw for the first time ever in November 2014.

The months before had seen a frenzy of action among the four other confederations as they each hosted their qualifying tournaments. It was a straightforward job for respective champions USA, Brazil, New Zealand and Nigeria, all so regularly dominant forces on their continents; joining them in reaching Canada 2015 were Mexico and Colombia, and maiden finals nations Cameroon, Cote d'Ivoire and Costa Rica.

The last piece of the jigsaw is Canada, of course. As hosts, the Canucks automatically qualified for the tournament they have graced five times previously. The nation expects their team to go all the way this time, but supporters of the 23 others have high hopes too. Only one nation can win, but after the manifold efforts that have gone into getting this far, all will do their utmost to make their country proud.

Left: **Switzerland's Ana Maria Crnogorcevic (13) jumps for the ball against Danish keeper Stina Lykke Petersen. The Group 3 qualifying game ended 1–1, the only goal conceded and points dropped by Switzerland on their way to Canada 2015.**

Right: **The United States' Carli Lloyd is congratulated by Megan Rapinoe. Lloyd scored five goals and won the Golden Ball for best player at the 2014 CONCACAF Women's Championship.**

THE VENUES

From coast to coast, in six vibrant host cities surrounded by stunning scenery, Canada provides the perfect setting for the FIFA Women's World Cup 2015.

Extending from the Atlantic to the Pacific and northward to the Arctic, Canada's enormous landmass (the second-largest country in the world, behind Russia) encompasses 10 provinces, three territories and six time zones. Its population of 35 million is officially bilingual, ethnically diverse, and warmly welcoming. And its awe-inspiring natural geography makes it the perfect destination for landscape lovers and al-fresco adventurers.

Matches at the FIFA Women's World Cup 2015 will be played in six dynamic cities stretching from coast to coast. Some of the venues for 2015 are home to both soccer and gridiron football teams and all 52 games will be played on artificial turf, rather than grass, fields that meet the FIFA 2-Star football turf requirements (ensuring the highest playing performance for professional-level football) to guarantee an equitable standard of surface for all teams. And goal-line technology will be in place for the first time ever in a women's competition.

The standard of host stadia is high too, with the climax set to be played in the nation's premier soccer venue, the beautiful BC Place, home to Whitecaps FC soccer team in Vancouver, British Columbia. Reopened in 2011 after a $563 million makeover and the installation of the largest cable-supported retractable roof of its kind anywhere, BC Place lies in the midst of Vancouver's entertainment district and is set to host nine matches including the final.

Eleven games, including the tournament opener, will kick off in front of the green and gold seats of the Edmonton Eskimos in the Commonwealth Stadium, Edmonton, Alberta – a fitting opening venue given the phenomenal support for soccer in the city. The folk of Edmonton turned out in record numbers – 47,784 – to witness Canada taking on USA in the final of the first-ever FIFA U-19 Women's World Championship in 2002, still the biggest crowd at a FIFA youth women's match.

Heading eastwards to the "cultural cradle of Canada" we reach another host venue, Winnipeg Stadium which opened in 2013. Winnipeg, Manitoba, hosted Canada's first-ever women's national team camp, on Canada Day, 1 July 1986, and the first women's home international friendly on 23 July 1990.

Ottawa, Ontario, is the country's capital and a hotbed for the game offering leagues for players of all ages and skill levels. Ottawa's stadium was renovated in July 2014 and while it is one of the smaller venues, its fans will no doubt create a fantastic atmosphere.

Moving on to Montreal, Quebec, we reach the imposing Olympic Stadium otherwise known as "The Big O". Host to Major League Soccer team Montreal Impact, this iconic landmark will be a lively venue for nine games, including a semi-final.

Last and furthest east, but certainly not least, is Moncton, New Brunswick, Canada's first officially bilingual city and host to seven matches. Moncton Stadium, set on the campus of the Universite de Moncton, is a compact arena but ideal for creating a buzz and sense of occasion.

This is North America's third FIFA Women's World Cup but Canada's first and it is more than ready.

Below: **Canada will play China PR in the tournament opener in the Commonwealth Stadium, Edmonton.**

VANCOUVER

British Columbia

B.C. Place Stadium

Capacity: **54,500**

WINNIPEG

Manitoba

Winnipeg Stadium

Capacity: **40,000**

MONTREAL

Quebec

Olympic Stadium

Capacity: **66,308**

MONCTON

New Brunswick

Moncton Stadium

Capacity: **20,725**

EDMONTON

Alberta

Commonwealth Stadium

Capacity: **56,302**

OTTAWA

Ontario

Lansdowne Stadium

Capacity: **40,000**

CANADA 2015
FIFA
WOMEN'S WORLD CUP

FIFA WOMEN'S WORLD CUP
CANADA 2015

THE DRAW

Officials, coaches and media came together in the culturally rich surroundings of the Canadian Museum of History in Ottawa in December 2014 to witness a crucial part of the FIFA Women's World Cup 2015 – the draw.

Performing the task in front of a worldwide television audience and a packed auditorium were Jerome Valcke, FIFA Secretary General, and Tatjana Haenni, FIFA Head of Women's Football, assisted by a selection of inspirational Canadian sporting stars.

There were gasps almost immediately as it transpired that hosts Canada, their distinctive red ball deliberately plucked out first, would face coach John Herdman's former charges New Zealand.

"They represent a lot to me," was his beaming response. "So to have the opportunity to share a moment with them in Canada is really great."

China PR were also in the mix in Group A and they will share Canada's own great moment when the two kick off the tournament in Edmonton.

Current holders Japan bagged a group with three first-timers, while England were picked alongside their 2011 adversaries, France. Meanwhile 2007 winners Germany were matched up with their UEFA Women's Euro 2013 final opponents, Norway.

The biggest drama, though, came when USA, Sweden, former Asian champions Australia and African giants Nigeria were drawn together to earn Group D the inevitable "group of death" moniker.

Sweden coach Pia Sundhage, who led USA to silver in 2011, was optimistic. "It's good to play against the best teams in the group stage, though," she said. "We're looking at it positively."

Below: **Tatjana Haenni and Jerome Valcke, in the centre, oversee the completed draw for the FIFA Women's World Cup Canada 2015 in front of a rapt audience.**

Right: **An Officer of the Royal Canadian Mounted Police carries the 45cm tall, FIFA Women's World Cup trophy at the draw.**

MATCH SCHEDULE

Watch the games, fill in the scores and follow the unfolding drama and excitement of the FIFA Women's World Cup Canada 2015.

GROUP A

6 JUNE	16:00	EDMONTON	
CANADA		**CHINA PR**	
6 JUNE	19:00	EDMONTON	
NEW ZEALAND		**NETHERLANDS**	
11 JUNE	16:00	EDMONTON	
CHINA PR		**NETHERLANDS**	
11 JUNE	19:00	EDMONTON	
CANADA		**NEW ZEALAND**	
15 JUNE	18:30	WINNIPEG	
CHINA PR		**NEW ZEALAND**	
15 JUNE	19:30	MONTREAL	
NETHERLANDS		**CANADA**	

TEAM	P	W	D	L	F	A	PTS

GROUP B

7 JUNE	13:00	OTTAWA	
NORWAY		**THAILAND**	
7 JUNE	16:00	OTTAWA	
GERMANY		**COTE D'IVOIRE**	
11 JUNE	16:00	OTTAWA	
GERMANY		**NORWAY**	
11 JUNE	19:00	OTTAWA	
COTE D'IVOIRE		**THAILAND**	
15 JUNE	15:00	WINNIPEG	
THAILAND		**GERMANY**	
15 JUNE	17:00	MONCTON	
COTE D'IVOIRE		**NORWAY**	

TEAM	P	W	D	L	F	A	PTS

GROUP C

8 JUNE	16:00	VANCOUVER	
CAMEROON		**ECUADOR**	
8 JUNE	19:00	VANCOUVER	
JAPAN		**SWITZERLAND**	
12 JUNE	16:00	VANCOUVER	
SWITZERLAND		**ECUADOR**	
12 JUNE	19:00	VANCOUVER	
JAPAN		**CAMEROON**	
16 JUNE	15:00	EDMONTON	
SWITZERLAND		**CAMEROON**	
16 JUNE	16:00	WINNIPEG	
ECUADOR		**JAPAN**	

TEAM	P	W	D	L	F	A	PTS

GROUP D

8 JUNE	15:00	WINNIPEG	
SWEDEN		**NIGERIA**	
8 JUNE	18:30	WINNIPEG	
USA		**AUSTRALIA**	
12 JUNE	16:00	WINNIPEG	
AUSTRALIA		**NIGERIA**	
12 JUNE	19:00	WINNIPEG	
USA		**SWEDEN**	
16 JUNE	17:00	VANCOUVER	
NIGERIA		**USA**	
16 JUNE	18:00	EDMONTON	
AUSTRALIA		**SWEDEN**	

TEAM	P	W	D	L	F	A	PTS

GROUP E

9 JUNE	16:00	MONTREAL		
SPAIN		COSTA RICA		
9 JUNE	19:00	MONTREAL		
BRAZIL		KOREA REPUBLIC		
13 JUNE	16:00	MONTREAL		
BRAZIL		SPAIN		
13 JUNE	19:00	MONTREAL		
KOREA REPUBLIC		COSTA RICA		
17 JUNE	19:00	OTTAWA		
KOREA REPUBLIC		SPAIN		
17 JUNE	20:00	MONCTON		
COSTA RICA		BRAZIL		

TEAM	P	W	D	L	F	A	PTS

GROUP F

9 JUNE	14:00	MONCTON		
FRANCE		ENGLAND		
9 JUNE	17:00	MONCTON		
COLOMBIA		MEXICO		
13 JUNE	14:00	MONCTON		
FRANCE		COLOMBIA		
13 JUNE	17:00	MONCTON		
ENGLAND		MEXICO		
17 JUNE	16:00	OTTAWA		
MEXICO		FRANCE		
17 JUNE	16:00	MONTREAL		
ENGLAND		COLOMBIA		

TEAM	P	W	D	L	F	A	PTS

ROUND OF 16

(39)	20 JUNE	16:00	OTTAWA	
1B				3ACD

(37)	20 JUNE	17:30	EDMONTON	
2A				2C

(41)	21 JUNE	14:00	MONCTON	
1E				2D

(40)	21 JUNE	16:00	MONTREAL	
1F				2E

(44)	21 JUNE	16:30	VANCOUVER	
1A				3CDE

(43)	22 JUNE	17:00	OTTAWA	
2B				2F

(38)	22 JUNE	18:00	EDMONTON	
1D				3BEF

(42)	23 JUNE	19:00	VANCOUVER	
1C				3ABF

QUARTER-FINALS

(46)	26 JUNE	16:00	MONTREAL	
W39				W40

(45)	26 JUNE	19:30	OTTAWA	
W37				W38

(47)	27 JUNE	14:00	EDMONTON	
W41				W42

(48)	27 JUNE	16:30	VANCOUVER	
W43				W44

SEMI-FINALS

(49)	30 JUNE	19:00	MONTREAL	
W45				W46

(50)	1 JULY	17:00	EDMONTON	
W47				W48

THIRD PLACE

	4 JULY	14:00	EDMONTON	
L49				L50

FINAL

	5 JULY	16:00	VANCOUVER	
W49				W50

MEET THE TEAMS

To perform and excel on the world stage is surely the dream of any player, and success at the FIFA Women's World Cup represents the apex of a female footballer's career. For some teams making their first appearances at the tournament, qualification was an achievement in itself; for others nothing but outright victory will suffice. From established masters of the elite game to ambitious new stars ready to shine, here are the 24 sides that make up Canada 2015.

Japan's ecstatic players revel in the moment of being crowned the best in the world, in Frankfurt, in July 2011. Four years on, with 23 other sides vying for that title, can they repeat that success?

The seating at Edmonton's Commonwealth Stadium boasts the colours of the Edmonton Eskimos Canadian Football League team.

CANADA
2015

FIFA
WOMEN'S WORLD CUP

TM©

GROUP A

All eyes will be on Canada's opener in Edmonton against China PR, the Canucks the victors in the two sides' only previous FIFA Women's World Cup meeting, in 2003. China have beaten New Zealand twice before while the Netherlands are an unknown quantity and could be the dark horse of the group.

CANADA
CAN THE HOSTS GO ALL THE WAY?

As hosts of the FIFA Women's World Cup 2015, Canada were spared the pressures of the CONCACAF qualifying tournament. The Canucks, though, will still be expected to hit the ground running when the tournament kicks off on home soil in June.

COACH

JOHN HERDMAN
From County Durham, this charismatic Englishman has experience of senior tournament football, having coached New Zealand in two editions of the FIFA Women's World Cup and at the 2008 Olympics in Beijing. Noted for instilling a professional mentality and learning environment into the Football Ferns. Took over Canada after the departure of Carolina Morace in 2011 and was nominated for FIFA coach of the year in 2012. Touted as a possible replacement for England manager Hope Powell in 2013 but since signed a long-term contract with Canada until 2020. Prepared to give youth a chance and has declared that hosts Canada have to go all out to lift the World Cup in 2015.

Having finished an impressive fourth in the FIFA Women's World Cup 2003 and with a rising reputation, Canada surprisingly stuttered in the following editions, despite the promise offered by clinching the CONCACAF title in 2010.

However, under Englishman John Herdman, who took over at the helm soon after the FIFA Women's World Cup 2011, they quickly returned to winning ways.

A historic gold medal performance at the Pan American Games in Mexico in 2011 gave Canada the chance to catch their breath after it was knocked out of them in their pointless FIFA Women's World Cup that year. And their subsequent display in the London 2012 Olympic Games showed the world that the elite teams still have the capacity to breathe new life into the sport. Canada's performance in an exhilarating end-to-end Olympic semi-final defeat by neighbours and rivals the USA at Old Trafford will live long in the memory of football fans of all nations.

And as the Canucks filed on to the pitch at Wembley Stadium to collect their medals after beating France to bronze, there was genuine appreciation for their efforts that summer. They will look to up their medal count this summer and have prepared with friendlies against the top teams in the world, including Germany, the USA and Japan.

The Canucks team will experience the mixed intensity of pressure and support that being the host side brings.

KEY PLAYER

CHRISTINE SINCLAIR
Born: 12 June 1983

Earning her first senior appearance aged 16, Sinclair has gone on to win more than 200 caps for her country. Big, strong and determined, she is a clinical finisher from any part of the park. In 2010 she became only the 10th female player to score 100 international goals. Described by her coach John Herdman as a "Rolls Royce" of a player, the Canucks' captain leads by example. Top scorer and a flag bearer for Canada at the close of the London 2012 Olympics, she remains humble despite her legendary status in the women's game. Has won 12 Canadian soccer player of the year titles plus nominations for FIFA Women's World Player of the Year. Signed for Portland Thorns (returning to the city where she had a stellar college career) in the US National Women's Soccer League in 2013.

WOMEN'S WORLD CUP RECORD

Year	Venue	Result
1991	China	Did not qualify
1995	Sweden	Group stage (3rd, Group B)
1999	USA	Group stage (3rd, Group C)
2003	USA	Fourth Place
2007	China	Group stage (3rd, Group C)
2011	Germany	Group stage (4th, Group A)

The squad's youngsters were kept on their toes when they featured in the FIFA U-20 Women's World Cup 2014 in Canada. A handful of the players – like impressive centre-back Kadeisha Buchanan – who made it to the quarter-finals of that competition are in with a shout of the senior tournament. Their experience of playing in front of expectant home crowds will be invaluable.

And while Herdman has been keen to blood teenagers in his senior set-up – four players were aged 18 and under in the 2–1 friendly loss to Germany in June 2014 – the core of his team played in the FIFA Women's World Cup 2011.

Those veterans will offer stability to the squad but Herdman has called for the 12th player to step up in 2015. "Don't just come and watch us," he told Canadians. "Come out and support us and help us win the FIFA Women's World Cup."

LOOK OUT FOR

ERIN MCLEOD
Born: 26 February 1983
Position: Goalkeeper

Super shot-stopper who has been playing football since the age of four. Acrobatic, quick and commanding, she is a safe pair of hands and has the confidence and trust of her defensive line. Won Olympic bronze in 2012 and her positional play, reliability and decision-making were praised in the subsequent technical report. Named in the All-Time Canada XI women's team in 2012, she was the Canucks' player of the match in the 2–1 friendly loss to Germany in June 2014.

JESSIE FLEMING
Born: 11 March 1998
Position: Midfielder

Aged 15 when she made her senior debut in December 2013 and has represented Canada in the 2014 FIFA U-17 and U-20 Women's World Cups. A fine athlete who started playing football aged three, she loves to get on the ball, reads the game superbly and can pick a pass and link play. Tasted tournament action on home soil with the U-20s in 2014 and will not be overawed if Herdman gives her the chance in the senior competition this summer.

DESIREE SCOTT
Born: 31 July 1987
Position: Midfielder

Experienced player who relishes her nickname "Destroyer" and is another product of Canada's youth system. Debuted for the seniors aged 22 in February 2010 and was part of the Cyprus Cup winning side that year. Featured in the FIFA Women's World Cup 2011 but has flourished under Herdman. A key member of the Pan American Games gold medal side that year and shone at London 2012. In 2014, joined Notts County in the English FA Women's Super League.

CHINA PR

YOUNG STEEL ROSES LOOKING TO BLOSSOM THIS SUMMER

Some nations are perennial performers at the FIFA Women's World Cup and China PR were one of those until they missed out in 2011. Now they are back – but how will the Steel Roses fare in Canada?

COACH

HAO WEI

Appointed head coach after China missed out on qualification to both the FIFA Women's World Cup 2011 and London 2012 Olympics – so the heat was on in the AFC Women's Asian Cup. The former defender rode the challenge, staying calm as China finished third and qualified for 2015. Still only 38, he boasts a wealth of playing experience in the Chinese league and has coached men but seems to be relishing his involvement in the women's game. Travelled to the north-east of England in July 2014 to meet English FA Women's Super League side Sunderland Ladies and share ideas on football development.

China's record in the top women's tournament is a decent one; they have never come away from the biggest stage of all without reaching at least the quarter-finals and in 1999 they almost took the title – only to lose on penalties to the USA.

Their form has fluctuated since those heady days and they were absent completely when Japan pipped them to a berth in the FIFA Women's World Cup 2011, but they have consciously rebuilt with youth and so they go into 2015 with the hopes of a nation behind them after gaining qualification with a best finish in the AFC Women's Asian Cup since 2008.

In May 2014, the tournament in Vietnam was the key to qualification in Asia, and China automatically booked their place in Canada when they finished runners-up in their group.

Beating relative minnows Thailand and Myanmar then drawing with a tough Korea Republic meant it was job done, but China, with their proud tradition in the women's game, wanted to achieve more. Coach Hao Wei's side also wanted to get a winning momentum underway in the lead-up to Canada 2015.

The Steel Roses did their utmost to remain unbeaten but lost 2–1 to old rivals Japan in the semi-finals, in a tense match that was agonizingly settled by a goal in

The new-look China PR team have the honour of opening the tournament against Canada in Edmonton.

KEY PLAYER

YANG LI
Born: 31 January 1991

They call her the new Sun Wen and she is most definitely a goal-getter in the mould of China's all-time highest-scoring legend. Strong in the air, she has a lethal technique but is no showboater and can grab scrappy goals from close range or pounce to punish sloppy passing. First came to prominence at the invitational Four Nations Tournament which China won in 2014. Established herself in the senior side during the Algarve Cup and showed her goalscoring prowess when it mattered in the qualifying competition for Canada 2015, the AFC Women's Asian Cup. The Jiangsu Huatai player finished the tournament as joint top scorer with six goals including the winner against Korea Republic that saw China take third place overall.

WOMEN'S WORLD CUP RECORD

Year	Venue	Result
1991	China	Quarter-finalists
1995	Sweden	Fourth place
1999	USA	Runners-up
2003	USA	Quarter-finalists
2007	China	Quarter-finalists
2011	Germany	Did not qualify

the dying moments of extra time.

They still left a hot and humid Ho Chi Minh City with their heads held high, though, after beating a talented Korea Republic by a late-late goal in the match for third place three days later.

Hao showed faith in youngsters, fielding a side whose average age was 23 in the competition, and believes that China have a team for the future on their hands.

"It gives me hope that there's a great foundation to improve upon in the future," said Hao, who then added that work to plot China's build-up to Canada was underway.

Three years of working on their game as a group has led to them gaining a sound grasp of their individual and collective defensive duties. When deployed, it is a system that can contain threatening opponents, while they have the additional armoury to hit teams swiftly and with potency, on the break.

Narrowly failing to go beyond the quarter-finals of the Asian Games in September 2014 is perhaps a sign that China are still a work in progress. Canada 2015 will certainly be another yardstick for this developing team.

LOOK OUT FOR

ZHANG YUE
Born: 30 September 1990
Position: Goalkeeper

Dependable and intelligent keeper whose height and clever positioning make her a tough opponent to beat. Showed her potential at the FIFA U-20 Women's World Cup 2008 and has gone on to become first choice No. 1, gaining further high-intensity experience at annual friendly tournaments such as the Four Nations invitational and Algarve Cup. Kept three clean sheets in group play at the AFC Women's Asian Cup in May 2014, ultimately conceding just three goals in five matches.

WU HAIYAN
Born: 26 February 1993
Position: Defender

Influential skipper who commands the defence from the centre but can do a job at right-back too. Calm and collected, she plays with a maturity beyond her years and is a reliable leader. Made her senior debut in 2011 and gained valuable tournament experience at the FIFA U-20 Women's World Cup 2012. Key player in China's Algarve Cup campaign in 2014 and ever-present in the AFC Women's Asian Cup matches that secured China's qualification for Canada 2015.

MA XIAOXU
Born: 5 June 1988
Position: Forward

Dubbed a teenage sensation before China's last FIFA Women's World Cup outing when they hosted the tournament, "Lady Wayne Rooney" will celebrate her 27th birthday in Canada. Scored the goals that saw China win the AFC Women's Asian Cup in 2006 and won the Golden Ball and Shoe at the FIFA U-20 Women's World Championship the same year. Has also played in Sweden's highly-respected Damallsvenskan. With such an effective background she could now be ready to fulfil her considerable promise.

NEW ZEALAND

FOOTBALL FERNS READY TO REALIZE POTENTIAL

New Zealand have made impressive strides since the FIFA Women's World Cup in 2011. As they head to their third consecutive finals, the Football Ferns will be ambitious to do more than make up the numbers.

COACH

TONY READINGS
Played at non-league level for AFC Wimbledon in his homeland of England before moving to play with North Shore United in New Zealand. Was assistant to current Canada coach John Herdman at the FIFA Women's World Cup in 2011, as well as the 2008 Olympics. The 39-year-old has a great understanding of the potential of his young squad, having managed the Junior Football Ferns at the FIFA U-20 Women's World Cup in 2010. Took full control of the senior side in the lead-up to the London 2012 Olympic Games where they registered their first international finals tournament win with a 3–1 victory over Cameroon.

Rather, New Zealand will hope to better their current record of having collected one point in the competition – against Mexico in 2011 – by building upon more recent outings against the best nations in the world.

Notable results have included a quarter-final berth in the London 2012 Olympics, where they lost 2–0 to eventual winners USA, and victories over Brazil and China PR to lift the inaugural Valais Women's Cup in Switzerland in September 2013.

The Ferns also went on to narrowly lose 2–1 to world champions Japan in a friendly in May 2014, before drawing in a double-header with Brazil the following month.

They staked their place in the FIFA Women's World Cup in October 2014 with a convincing show in their qualification tournament, the OFC Women's Nations Cup. The Kiwis scored 30 goals without reply in three games, although plucky hosts Papua New Guinea kept the score down to 3–0 in their encounter with Tony Readings' side, who won the tournament to make it a record fifth OFC Women's Nations Cup title.

Skipper Abby Erceg said afterwards that the competition had been a good test for the Ferns and an indicator of the areas that needed to be worked on ahead of their arrival in Canada.

"I think the most exciting thing heading

The Football Ferns of New Zealand are super fit and always give their all, to the very end.

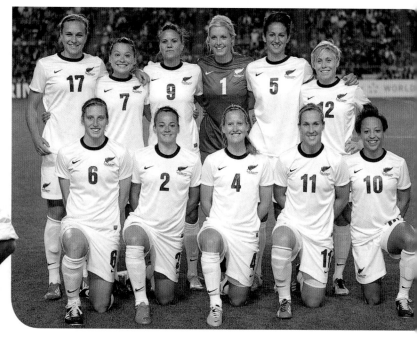

KEY PLAYER

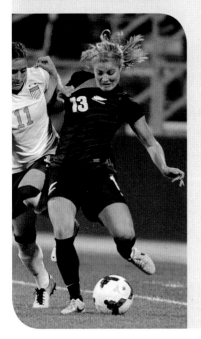

ROSIE WHITE
Born: 6 June 1993

Strong, direct striker who likes to wear the No. 13 shirt and was regarded as a football prodigy when she hit a hat-trick against Colombia in the FIFA U-17 Women's World Cup 2008. Scored three more for the Junior Football Ferns against hosts Chile at the FIFA U-20 edition just 18 days later. Fast-tracked into the seniors, the multiple New Zealand Football young player of the year winner made her debut as a 15-year-old against China in 2009. Her performances at the FIFA U-20 Women's World Cup 2010 earned her a scholarship at the University of California, Los Angeles, where she has learnt, grown – and scored goals. Awarded the Golden Ball for best player in the OFC Women's Nations Cup, she has a raft of tournament experience.

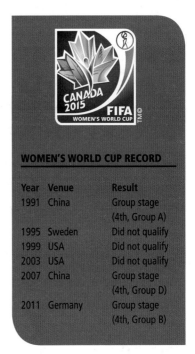

WOMEN'S WORLD CUP RECORD

Year	Venue	Result
1991	China	Group stage (4th, Group A)
1995	Sweden	Did not qualify
1999	USA	Did not qualify
2003	USA	Did not qualify
2007	China	Group stage (4th, Group D)
2011	Germany	Group stage (4th, Group B)

to this World Cup is the real prospect of us being a true threat to the top nations and seeing how far we can push ourselves and our performance," she added.

As the top nation in Oceania, New Zealand are definitely a dominant force within their own confederation, and their gutsy approach and competitive nature typifies their attitude to the game. But that style is still developing as players come together for more frequent international camps, friendlies and tournaments, and an increasing number garner experience of league football in Europe and Asia.

As Canada 2015 draws near, other nations in the world are starting to notice that the Kiwis' athletic, never-say-die attitude is now complemented by greater finesse and tactical awareness.

With a string of testing friendlies taking the Ferns all the way through to the summer, Oceania's number one side should be ready to set new records for all the world to see.

LOOK OUT FOR

ALI RILEY
Born: 30 October 1987
Position: Defender

Athletic wing-back who was born in California but is eligible to represent New Zealand because her dad is a Kiwi. Has spent the majority of her career in America, most notably with FC Gold Pride in the Women's Professional Soccer league and then Western New York Flash in their WPS Championship-winning season of 2011. Veteran of two FIFA Women's World Cups and two Olympics, she joined LdB FC Malmo, now FC Rosengard, in Sweden in 2012, winning titles with both.

ABBY ERCEG
Born: 20 November 1989
Position: Defender

Captain since 2013, she debuted in 2006 and has since been a virtual ever-present, becoming the first player, male or female, to win 100 caps for New Zealand. Followed her New Zealand Football young player of the year award in 2007 with the NZF players' player accolade in 2011. A true leader on and off the field, she is another Fern who enjoys her club football overseas, having competed in both the Frauen-Bundesliga in Germany and the USA's National Women's Soccer League.

AMBER HEARN
Born: 28 November 1984
Position: Forward

This powerful "fox in the box" has played in England (Doncaster Belles and Arsenal), Canada (Ottawa Fury) and Germany (FF USV Jena). Made her senior international debut in February 2004 and went on to be named NZF women's player of the year. Has appeared in two Olympics and one FIFA Women's World Cup for the Football Ferns, netting against Japan in both tournaments. Top-scored at the 2014 OFC Women's Nations Cup to maintain her status as New Zealand's most prolific striker.

NETHERLANDS
ORANJE LEEUWINNEN SET TO MAKE THEIR WORLD BOW

The Netherlands had to play their hearts out to make it to Canada 2015, competing not only in their qualifying group but in four high-pressure play-off matches. They will savour their world bow, but how well can they expect to do this summer?

COACH

ROGER REIJNERS
Played in midfield and won four caps for the Netherlands under-21s. Spent his club career with professional sides Fortuna Sittard and MVV Maastricht. Playing career ended in 1995 but he went on to become first-team head coach at both of his former clubs. Succeeded the successful Vera Pauw as national women's team coach in November 2010 and is keen on possession-based football. The 51-year-old led the side through to qualification for the UEFA Women's Euro 2013 and the FIFA Women's World Cup 2015, with a contract in place until the Olympic Games in 2016.

The Dutch fared poorly in their last big tournament, the UEFA Women's Euro 2013. They finished bottom of a tough group, a disappointing showing after having reached the last four of the competition in 2009, their first outing in a major finals. They bounced back in November 2014, however, when they concluded an impressive FIFA Women's World Cup qualification campaign with a guaranteed place in the finals and their confidence on the big stage restored.

"After the last European Championship we discussed what we wanted and what we needed to improve," said head coach Roger Reijners. "And you see that we really have taken steps since the beginning of this year."

Indeed, with such a strong defence, creative midfield and clinical attack they might even go on to spring a few surprises in Canada. Reijners' players, who mostly compete in the BeNe League that features teams from Belgium and the Netherlands, certainly showed a steely resolve to take on Europe's best in their bid to reach the FIFA tournament in the Land of the Maple Leaf. All told, group champions Norway were the only side to beat them during their long qualification campaign and in the final tally a mere two points were all that separated the two.

Second was not enough to automatically qualify for Canada but the Dutch were

They may have booked their place to the party later than most, but the Dutch will be raring to go, come June.

KEY PLAYER

VIVIANNE MIEDEMA
Born: 15 July 1996

Described by coaches and media alike as a "phenomenon", this 18-year-old is one of the hottest prospects in Europe. Made her senior debut as a substitute against Albania in the first of the Netherlands' FIFA Women's World Cup qualification matches and went on to top-score with 16 goals in the campaign. Has two great feet and can turn even half-chances into goals, but her celebrations can be remarkably understated. Spearheaded the Netherlands' first major women's title triumph, the 2014 UEFA European Women's Under-19 Championship, and was named the tournament's Golden Player after scoring six goals. Highest scorer in the BeNe League in 2014 with sc Heerenveen and joined German Frauen-Bundesliga club FC Bayern Munich that summer.

WOMEN'S WORLD CUP RECORD

The Dutch defeated Scotland and Italy in the UEFA play-offs, both played over two legs, to bag a place at their first ever FIFA Women's World Cup.

among the four best runners-up and they maintained their momentum in the play-offs that followed. Scotland were beaten home and away to set up two do-or-die encounters with Italy. "It's about playing at the World Cup for the first time ever," said record goalscorer Manon Melis. "It

will be all or nothing." Dutch teenager Vivianne Miedema certainly gave the matches all she had and her three goals in both the resulting 1–1 draw in front of 13,100 at Den Haag and 2–1 win in the return in Verona were enough to see the Netherlands through.

It will have pleased the Dutch that Miedema was so instrumental in their historic feat. The teenager was key to the Netherlands' victory in the UEFA European Women's Under-19 Championship in 2014 and that crown bodes well for this nation's future prospects. The Netherlands today are strong, physical and football savvy. With the UEFA Women's Euro due to take place in the Netherlands in 2017, the eyes of the world are on this ever-improving women's football nation.

LOOK OUT FOR

LOES GEURTS
Born: 12 January 1986
Position: Goalkeeper

Became first choice in 2006 after the retirement of record cap-holder Marleen Wissink. Now the rock at the heart of the Dutch defence, she is a calm and organizing influence. An able shot-stopper who is brave and effective in one-on-ones. Developed her skills as a child against her brothers, using a bus shelter for a goal! Won Eredivisie Vrouwen titles with AZ Alkmaar before playing in Sweden's Damallsvenskan with Vittsjo GIK and Goteborg FC.

LIEKE MARTENS
Born: 16 December 1992
Position: Forward

Technically smart right-footed footballer with power and pace who most often operates on the left side. She has played for sc Heerenveen and VVV-Venlo in the Dutch Eredivisie Vrouwen and for Standard de Liege in the Belgian Women's Elite League, scoring as they won the BeNe SuperCup two years in a row. Has also played in Germany with FCR 2001 Duisburg and for Goteborg FC of the Swedish Damallsvenskan.

MANON MELIS
Born: 31 August 1986
Position: Forward

Daughter of former Feyenoord and Den Haag attacker Harry, she is one of the fastest players in the women's game and a clinical finisher who is a reliable goalscorer with more than a century of caps and counting. Has also shown her world-class credentials at club level in the highly competitive Swedish Damallsvenskan, topping the scoring charts three times, winning three titles and claiming individual accolades during spells with LdB FC Malmo and Goteborg FC.

The rejuvenated Lansdowne Stadium is home to Ottawa Fury FC of the North American Soccer League.

GROUP B

Two newcomers and two old foes combine here
and, while all the games will be watched eagerly,
anticipation is split between waiting to see who will
come out on top on 11 June when Germany face
Norway in Ottawa, and Cote d'Ivoire and Thailand
meet there just hours later.

GERMANY
GIANTS OF THE GAME GO FOR GOLD

Germany are an ever-present nation in the FIFA Women's World Cup. One of only four to have lifted the trophy in its 24-year history, they have won the tournament twice. Could Germany make it a trio of titles in 2015?

COACH

SILVIA NEID

Former midfielder Neid enjoyed a glittering career as a player, winning a host of league and cup titles and captaining Germany to European glory in 1989, scoring as they retained the title two years later. Was assistant to successful Germany coach Tina Theune from 1996 to 2005 and also coached at youth level, winning several UEFA and FIFA tournaments with the under-18s and 19s. Took over the senior side in 2005. A runner-up in the FIFA Women's World Cup as a player, she won the competition as Germany coach in 2007 and has overseen two UEFA Women's Euro title triumphs. Has been crowned world coach of the year by FIFA and values honesty and discipline in her work.

There is every chance they may do, given a sumptuous qualification campaign that saw them record a perfect 10 out of 10 victories. A remarkable 62 goals were scored, with just four conceded, and Germany's ticket to Canada was in the bag with a game to spare – they went on to finish eight points clear of second-placed Russia in September 2014.

Sandwiched inside that brilliant campaign was an Algarve Cup triumph in March 2014 which included a 3–0 win in the final over FIFA Women's World Cup holders Japan. Ironically, the Nadeshiko had ejected Germany from the FIFA Women's World Cup 2011 at the quarter-final stage, a knock-out on home soil that shocked onlookers and put paid to their hopes of qualification for the London 2012 Olympic Games.

There is little doubt that Silvia Neid's Germany are a different prospect these days and, given their recent run, the group we can expect to see in Canada are ripe for success. The first glimpse of their promise came in the UEFA Women's Euro 2013 in Sweden when injuries to key players meant that Neid needed to revamp her squad. A string of up-and-coming starlets such as Nadine Kessler and Dzsenifer Marozsan came into the fray and although they were far from imperious in the group stages they went on to make the final.

Often one of the most impressive things about any Germany team is not just the calibre of the starting eleven but also the quality of those players waiting in the wings.

KEY PLAYER

ANJA MITTAG
Born: 16 May 1985

Spearhead of the German attack who can play wide or operate in the No. 10 role. Bagged the winning goal in the UEFA Women's Euro 2013 final and top-scored for Germany in FIFA Women's World Cup qualification with 11 in nine matches. Also on target as Germany beat Japan in the Algarve Cup final. Was Golden Player in the 2004 UEFA European Women's Under-19 Championship and a member of Germany's FIFA Women's World Cup 2007 winning side. Suffered a dip by her own standards but since joining LdB FC Malmo (now FC Rosengard) in the Swedish Damallsvenskan in 2012 has roared back to form and was crowned league player and top scorer of that year and again in 2014.

WOMEN'S WORLD CUP RECORD

Year	Venue	Result
1991	China	Fourth place
1995	Sweden	Runners-up
1999	USA	Quarter-finalists
2003	USA	Winners
2007	China	Winners
2011	Germany	Quarter-finalists

There, they beat Norway 1–0 thanks to a blistering goal from substitute Anja Mittag, although veteran keeper and eventual UEFA player of the tournament Nadine Angerer had to make two crucial penalty saves to secure that eighth German Euro title.

The majority of that squad went on to pass their next big test – qualification for the FIFA Women's World Cup – prompting Neid to praise the tightness of the group. "We have a lot of strength in depth and we work well together," she said.

Given the players at Germany's disposal and, with FIFA U-20 Women's World Cup winners Sara Dabritz, Pauline Bremer and Lena Petermann knocking on the door, Neid does indeed have strength in depth. That, coupled with the impetus that a technically, tactically and physically competitive domestic league such as the Frauen-Bundesliga can offer a national side, suggests that this Germany could come of age in Canada.

LOOK OUT FOR

LEONIE MAIER
Born: 29 September 1992
Position: Defender

Hugely accomplished overlapping full-back who shone for Germany on their way to UEFA Women's Euro gold in 2013 despite having only made her senior debut in February of that year. Has solid experience of tournament play at youth level, winning the UEFA European Women's Championship with the under-17s in 2009 and the under-19s in 2011 before taking silver at the FIFA U-20 Women's World Cup 2012. Suffered anterior cruciate ligament injury in March 2014 but had gallantly battled back to play for FC Bayern Munich by October.

NADINE KESSLER
Born: 4 April 1988
Position: Midfielder

Crowned FIFA and UEFA best women's player in 2014 and not without reason – she is determined and creative, a genuine playmaker who can carve goals out of nothing. Former captain of the under-19s, she debuted for the seniors in 2010 and was a key member of the UEFA Women's Euro 2013-winning squad. Won the UEFA Women's Champions League with 1. FFC Turbine Potsdam and also as skipper at VfL Wolfsburg, alongside Germany midfield partner Lena Goessling.

DZSENIFER MAROZSAN
Born: 18 April 1992
Position: Midfielder

One of the most talented players of her generation, she boasts super skills, great control and accurate dead-ball delivery. Played her part in the UEFA Women's Euro 2013 tournament victory, scoring in the 1–0 semi-final win over Sweden. Hails from footballing stock – her father played for Hungary. Won the Golden Shoe and Silver Ball in the FIFA U-17 Women's World Cup in 2008 and Golden Ball in the U-20 edition in 2012. The youngest player to debut in the Frauen-Bundesliga with 1. FC Saarbrucken aged 14 years and seven months.

COTE D'IVOIRE

DEBUTANTS HAVE WHAT IT TAKES TO IMPRESS THE WORLD

Cote d'Ivoire may have been the surprise package of their FIFA Women's World Cup qualifying tournament in Namibia, but their potential was there for all to see. Now the world waits to see if these gifted debutants can spring yet more surprises in Canada.

COACH

CLEMENTINE TOURE

The 38-year-old was part of the coaching team that steered Equatorial Guinea to the African Women's Championship title in 2008. As head coach of her home nation she ironically saw her charges eliminate Equatorial Guinea on their way to qualification for the continental finals in 2014. Was one of three women coaches at the tournament proper – a first for the championship – and is very much a role model in the women's game in Africa. Made history when her side qualified for the FIFA Women's World Cup 2015 – and her tactical awareness was seen as a key component of that achievement.

The teams that are drawn against this West African side this summer will most definitely need to be on their toes – Les Elephantes have more than just technique in their lockers. Observers at their FIFA Women's World Cup qualifying competition, the African Women's Championship, trumpeted their movement, positional awareness, dogged determination and defensive nous too. And as even the best teams in the world know, opponents with such an array of abilities in their armoury can sometimes be the trickiest customers to overcome on the big stage, regardless of their history in the tournament.

Refreshingly for head coach Clementine Toure, the side that arrives in Canada will have no tournament back-story to live up to or put behind them because Cote d'Ivoire have never before qualified for a FIFA women's competition – at any level. So while these slight but sprightly players will have the steepest of learning curves to climb in Canada, they have nothing to prove and everything to gain, and so should play with freedom, joy and pride. They ought to be confident too after having reached Canada 2015 thanks to some promising displays in the African Women's Championship.

Having overcome Mali comfortably and then defending champions Equatorial

With all to play for and little to lose, Les Elephantes will learn a lot from their debut in Canada.

KEY PLAYER

ESTELLE JOSEE NAHI
Born: 29 May 1989

Inspirational skipper who can play on the wing or lead the line. Has the footballing nous and technique to be a genuine game-changer – as she showed in the qualifying competition for Canada 2015, the African Women's Championship in Namibia. Scored 13 minutes into her first game in the competition and went on to set up chances for others and score again as Cote d'Ivoire ultimately bagged the third African place on offer. Has experience of playing in the UEFA Women's Champions League with Serbian outfit Spartak Subotica and Russian side WFC Zvezda 2005, finding the back of the net for both clubs while representing them in the elite European competition. Will relish the chance to play against the best in the world.

WOMEN'S WORLD CUP RECORD

Finishing third at only their second African Women's Championship was enough to see Cote d'Ivoire make their debut at the finals in Canada.

Guinea in the preliminary rounds to qualify for the championship, they got off to a tricky start in the competition proper in Namibia in October 2014. Opening with a 4–2 loss to eventual winners (for a record seventh time) Nigeria was a set-back, but the Ivorians, who were making only their second-ever appearance at the championship, went on to beat hosts Namibia and draw with Zambia before losing in extra time to experienced African Women's Championship outfit Cameroon in the semi-final.

With Africa receiving three qualifying places at the FIFA Women's World Cup for the first time, however, there was still much to play for as Les Elephantes went into the third-place play-off with South Africa. Little wonder then that head coach Toure was mobbed by her joyous players after Ida Rebecca Guehai's 85th-minute goal secured victory over Banyana Banyana in Windhoek. It was a historic win, and the victory not only booked Cote d'Ivoire a ticket to Canada – it also announced their potential as one of the top nations in African women's football.

LOOK OUT FOR

KOKO ANGE N'GUESSAN
Born: 18 November 1990
Position: Midfielder/Forward

Described by observers as "too hot to handle" during the African Women's Championship as she combined with Nahi to pester opposition defences. Light on her feet, speedy and skilful, she is not the biggest member of the side but she plays without fear and ran South Africa ragged down both flanks in the play-off for the third FIFA Women's World Cup 2015 spot. Capable of scoring in key games. Was crowned 2013 Ivorian Football Federation player of the year.

IDA REBECCA GUEHAI
Born: 15 July 1994
Position: Midfielder

Goalscoring midfielder who bagged the vital winner in the African Women's Championship match against South Africa that booked her nation's place in their first-ever FIFA Women's World Cup. Also captained the under-20s in their bid to qualify for the FIFA U-20 Women's World Cup 2014. Is recognized as one of the best players in Cote d'Ivoire's Championnat National Feminin; top-scored in 2014 and was named Ivorian Football Federation player of the year.

TIA INES N'REHY
Born: 1 October 1993
Position: Forward

Instinctive striker with fine close control and aerial ability who was Cote d'Ivoire's leading scorer in their FIFA Women's World Cup 2015 qualifying campaign, with three goals. With bags of energy, she is an important cog in her nation's fluid attacking line. Another player with UEFA Women's Champions League experience; she scored on her debut in the competition for Serbian side Spartak Subotica in 2013, also hitting a hat-trick in the qualifiers in 2014.

NORWAY

PROUD WOMEN'S FOOTBALL NATION LOOKS BACK TO THE FUTURE

Norway were happy victors when they lifted the FIFA Women's World Cup trophy in Sweden in 1995. Twenty years on, the world wonders if history could repeat itself, this time in Canada.

COACH

EVEN PELLERUD

A great character in the game, he boasts more than 40 years' experience and a good deal of success too with his trademark style of direct football. Played and coached in the Norwegian men's top flight. Enjoyed immense triumphs with Norway in the 1990s, during which time he led them to FIFA Women's World Cup and UEFA Women's Euro gold. Took Canada to two FIFA Women's World Cups and won the Cyprus Cup with the Canucks in 2008. Coached Trinidad and Tobago for four years before returning to Norway for a second spell. Now in his 60s, he remains one of football's most energetic figures and the players say he has reinvigorated the squad.

The Grasshoppers will give it everything they have got – and that is quite a lot if you run the rule over their roster of exciting players and consider the pedigree of the coach who led them to qualification for 2015. Even Pellerud was at the helm when Norway achieved FIFA Women's World Cup glory in 1995 and since his return to the national set-up in 2012 he has shown his class yet again.

He has mixed precocious youngsters, such as the attack-minded Caroline Graham Hansen and Ada Stolsmo Hegerberg, in with experienced heads like keeper Ingrid Hjelmseth and defensive midfielder Maren Mjelde, to create a vibrant, competitive and cohesive Norway.

In the summer of 2013 they put in a stellar performance in the UEFA Women's Euro in Sweden, going all the way to the final where they pushed Germany to the limit before losing 1–0 after having two penalties saved.

They then brushed themselves down from that disappointment to put in a fine qualifying campaign for the FIFA Women's World Cup, eventually pipping the Netherlands to first place in Group 5. Norway lost just once along the way and that was in their final match, at home to the Netherlands four days after they had already booked their ticket thanks to an

Norwegian women's teams always have fighting spirit and little fear. The youngsters are not lacking in craft either.

KEY PLAYER

CAROLINE GRAHAM HANSEN
Born: 18 February 1995

A stand-out player of the women's game, the midfielder/forward has been labelled fearless, exciting and mature by seasoned observers. Still only 20 years old, she boasts amazing control and can cause mayhem in any back-line with her pacy dribbling and fierce runs. Was part of Norway's 2011 UEFA European Women's Under-19 Championship silver medal-winning side and debuted for the seniors that year. Went into the UEFA Women's Euro 2013 with just 16 caps but turned into one of their major players as Norway finished runners-up. A Norwegian league winner with Stabaek when she was just 15, she was snapped up by Tyreso FF of Sweden in 2013 and joined German side VfL Wolfsburg in 2014, experiencing valuable UEFA Women's Champions League competition with all three clubs.

WOMEN'S WORLD CUP RECORD

Year	Venue	Result
1991	China	Runners-up
1995	Sweden	Winners
1999	USA	Fourth place
2003	USA	Quarter-finalists
2007	China	Fourth place
2011	Germany	Group stage (3rd, Group D)

11–0 whitewash of Albania away in Durres.

Pellerud, a veteran of four FIFA Women's World Cups, was delighted to have steered a team to a fifth, describing the feeling of qualification as "fantastic". "We are confirmed as finals contenders," he added.

"That's phenomenal."

What perhaps is more remarkable is the way that Norway have come back into contention since a side hit by injury did the unthinkable and crashed out of the FIFA Women's World Cup 2011 at the group stage. Almost half of that 2011 squad remain and many played their part in Norway's success at UEFA Women's Euro 2013 and in their FIFA Women's World Cup qualification; the new faces have played beyond their years in both.

All will have learnt from their experiences and though a disappointingly low finish in the 2014 Algarve Cup suggests there is still work to be done, the foundations are there for Norway to become great again.

LOOK OUT FOR

INGRID HJELMSETH
Born: 10 April 1980
Position: Goalkeeper

A great communicator and brilliant distributor, this qualified software engineer is the safest of hands. Debuted in 2003 and has been No. 1 since 2009. Part of the Norway squad that finished second at the UEFA Women's Euro 2005 and third four years later. Named in the All-star UEFA Women's Euro 2013 squad and vital to qualification for Canada. Has won multiple domestic titles with SK Trondheims-Orn and Stabaek. Named 2013 Golden Ball winner by the Norwegian Football Association.

MAREN MJELDE
Born: 6 November 1989
Position: Defender/Midfielder

Solid defensive midfielder, she has turned in many accomplished performances at centre-back for her country but was also a revelation at right full-back in the UEFA Women's Euro 2013, deservedly making the All-star squad. Has experience of skippering sides in UEFA and FIFA youth tournaments and is a born leader. Hails from a footballing family (brother Erik is a professional) and played UEFA Women's Champions League football with 1. FFC Turbine Potsdam before moving to Sweden's Damallsvenskan.

ADA STOLSMO HEGERBERG
Born: 10 July 1995
Position: Forward

A striker with an eye for the spectacular as well as the speculative, she has great technique and sees and tries things that other players do not and dare not. Part of an exciting new generation, she debuted for the seniors in 2011 and was still a student during Norway's exciting run to the final of the UEFA Women's Euro 2013. Norwegian Players' Association young player of the year in 2011, she joined German outfit 1. FFC Turbine Potsdam in 2013 and then France's Olympique Lyonnais in 2014.

THAILAND
HISTORY MAKERS GEAR UP TO NEXT MILESTONE

Thailand have the honour of becoming the first south-east Asian country to qualify for a FIFA Women's World Cup. A relatively unknown quantity, their participation will be watched with interest.

COACH

NUENGRUETHAI SATHONGWIEN

A double history-maker – she is the first woman to lead the national side and in 2014 became the first to lead any Thai side to a senior FIFA World Cup tournament. A graduate of the Faculty of Sports Science of Kasetsart University, she was in charge of the Thai Women's Premier League side BG-CAS. Joined the national team as assistant coach in 2013 before taking over the reins in the lead-up to the AFC Women's Asian Cup. Also responsible for the youth set-up. Hailed qualification for Canada 2015 as a significant moment for the women's game in Thailand.

Not that that will be anything new to Thailand – they played the must-win AFC Women's Asian Cup match that secured their qualifying spot for Canada 2015 in front of a reported 18,000 fans on their rivals' home turf.

Success in the AFC Women's Asian Cup has secured the FIFA Women's World Cup places of five teams from the Asian confederation. Heading into the tournament in May 2014 Thailand were one of the favourites to clinch a place.

The Thais had won their group in the preliminary round, although they were tested to the limit by the Philippines. And they came into the cup competition having won gold for the fifth time in their history in the South East Asian Games the previous December by beating near neighbours Vietnam 2–1.

Once the AFC Women's Asian Cup kicked off, Thailand knew they would have to deal with the ambitions of fellow Group B sides Myanmar and the more experienced Korea Republic and China PR to keep their own FIFA Women's World Cup dreams alive.

It was a tough ask and Korea and China both got the better of head coach Nuengruethai Sathongwien's charges, who were unable to get a goal against their opponents in two high-scoring matches.

Midfielder Kanjana Sung-Ngoen and

No women's side from Thailand has reached a senior FIFA finals, so this is new territory for the team and the football-watching world.

KEY PLAYER

KANJANA SUNG-NGOEN
Born: 21 September 1986

Likes to patrol the right flank of the Thailand midfield but with her blistering pace can complement the frontline, scoring goals and setting up her team-mates with unselfish passes or a pinpoint dead-ball delivery. Has won gold with Thailand in the South East Asian Games and scored the two goals against Vietnam in the AFC Women's Asian Cup that booked their place in Canada; had also scored in the final of the ASEAN Football Federation Women's Championship to help Thailand win the tournament for the first time in 2011. Won rave reviews from spectators for her speed and skill during a spell in Japan with Nadeshiko League side Speranza FC in 2013.

WOMEN'S WORLD CUP RECORD

Newcomers Thailand are also the first side from the South East Asian region ever to qualify for a FIFA Women's World Cup finals.

defender Sritala Duangnapa both found the net for Thailand against Myanmar, though, and the Thais edged the match 2–1 to finish third in their group.

That crucial placing meant that if they could beat the third-place team in Group A they would still qualify for the FIFA Women's World Cup.

Given that the side they were due to face was Vietnam, who were both competition hosts and the outfit they had recently seen off in their quest to win gold in the South East Asian Games, this would undoubtedly be a test of nerves for Thailand.

It was one they passed with flying colours as Kanjana Sung-Ngoen again found the target with a brace in the second half to seal a 2–1 win over Vietnam in a vibrant Thong Nhat Stadium in Ho Chi Minh City.

"This victory and thereby qualifying for the World Cup is a very important milestone in our development," declared coach Sathongwien afterwards.

The coach was right. Thailand had written their names into FIFA Women's World Cup history – and now the world awaits their next chapter.

LOOK OUT FOR

DARUT CHANGPLOOK
Born: 3 February 1988
Position: Defender

Another who has enjoyed gold medal success in the ASEAN Football Federation Women's Championship and South East Asian Games, she played every minute of the AFC Women's Asian Cup to help Thailand qualify for Canada 2015. Easily spotted on the pitch with her dyed hair, she is a joy to watch too, full of running and capable of playing across the backline or in midfield, according to the flow of the game. Has the composure and skill to instigate attacks and likes to shoot when the chance arises.

TANEEKARN DANGDA
Born: 15 December 1992
Position: Forward

Part of the Thailand side that won gold in the South East Asian Games in December 2013. One of the tallest players in the Thailand squad, the 22-year-old gained valuable experience playing with Swedish side Ostersunds DFF during their promotion-chasing season of 2014 as part of a player exchange programme. Following in the footsteps of her brother Teerasil, who has come up through the ranks of the Thai men's national side.

NISA ROMYEN
Born: 18 January 1990
Position: Forward

Consistent goalscorer for her country at both youth and senior level; instinctively hits the target and is at her most dangerous from close range. Can grab a goal with her head or feet and was top scorer in the 2014 Asian Games. Hit eight goals to help Thailand in the preliminary rounds of the FIFA Women's World Cup qualifying competition, the AFC Women's Asian Cup, and played in every match as Thailand went on to secure a place in Canada.

BC Place in Vancouver, the main stadium for the 2010 Winter Olympics and now the venue for the final of the FIFA Women's World Cup 2015.

GROUP C

Here, current title-holders Japan are pitched with three debutants. It seems a foregone conclusion that the Nadeshiko will emerge in pole position, but the form book could still be rewritten and the opening two fixtures may indicate whether Switzerland, Cameroon or Ecuador are strong enough to challenge the champions.

JAPAN
CAN THE NADESHIKO RETAIN THEIR CROWN?

Japan lit up the sport in 2011 when they beat the USA in a thrill-a-minute final to become the first Asian side to win a senior World Cup. Will they have us all up on our feet again in 2015?

COACH

NORIO SASAKI

Played for NTT Kanto Soccer Club and retired from the game in his early 30s. Coached men early on in his career but joined Japan's women's structure as a youth coach in 2006. Took charge of the seniors in 2007 and first tasted success in the 2008 East Asian championship and the Olympics. Named FIFA women's football coach of the year in 2011 – justifiably so, given Japan's World Cup winning performance in Germany that year. Went on to lead the Nadeshiko to silver in the London 2012 Olympics. Known as a tough trainer with a sense of humour, a style that has paid off in spades thus far.

Humble, fast and dynamic, Japan certainly knocked the world for six by their refusal to lie down in the face of one of the greatest women's footballing nations.

Since that unforgettable FIFA Women's World Cup night in a sold-out stadium in Frankfurt in July 2011, Japan have gone on to claim their first-ever Olympic silver medal and their maiden AFC Women's Asian Cup title.

They were disappointed to lose their Asian Games title to Korea DPR in October 2014 but the Japanese knew they had at least secured the chance to defend their FIFA Women's World Cup title when they won in Asia in May. Topping their AFC Women's Asian Cup group secured their qualification for Canada, and they went

on to beat rivals China PR and Australia to claim the crown.

It seems remarkable now that Japan had not won the AFC Women's Asian Cup in their history until 2014 but it is perhaps a sign of how tight competition is between the teams in the confederation.

Their wins over China and Australia were certainly narrow, a single goal deciding both games with defender Azusa Iwashimizu's goals proving crucial in both matches.

Japan were without key names in the tournament, however, with club commitments depriving them of players of

Coach Norio Sasaki likes to rotate his starting line-ups; this team faced Korea DPR in the sixth East Asian Games.

KEY PLAYER

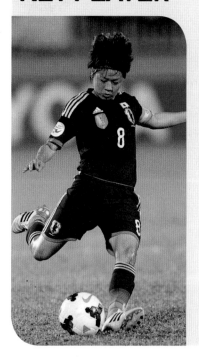

AYA MIYAMA
Born: 28 January 1985

The captain, she is a set-piece specialist with a dangerous right foot. Can boss a match with her vision and skill and is regularly hailed for her ability to think on her feet as well as her stamina and agility; always puts in a shift. Multiple Asian player of the year award winner and made the All-star team of the FIFA Women's World Cup 2011. So influential in the 2014 AFC Women's Asian Cup that she was named most valuable player of the tournament. Practices her free-kicks until they are perfect and says she is always thinking of set-plays and how to improve them. Has played in the USA and returned to Okayama Yunogo Belle in Japan's Nadeshiko League in 2010. Quite simply a world-class midfielder.

WOMEN'S WORLD CUP RECORD

Year	Venue	Result
1991	China	Group stage (4th, Group B)
1995	Sweden	Quarter-finalists
1999	USA	Group stage (4th, Group C)
2003	USA	Group stage (3rd, Group C)
2007	China	Group stage (3rd, Group C)
2011	Germany	Winners

the calibre of defender Yukari Kinga and attacker Shinobu Ohno who starred for English side Arsenal in 2014.

That said, coach Norio Sasaki seized the chance to bring up-and-coming footballers into the fray in Vietnam, with former under-age starlets Chinatsu Kira, Hikaru Naomoto and Ruka Norimatsu getting a run-out.

Sasaki said one of his tasks in the run-up to Canada was to blend Japan's young prospects in with established performers. One of the latter members of that elite group is striker Yuki Ogimi, a FIFA Women's World Cup winner who has strengthened her game by playing in Europe. "We are not satisfied just to have qualified because the goal is to win the tournament," she said. "And we want to show you our football and make you enjoy yourself!"

Fans everywhere will surely do that this summer when Japan once again showcase their skills on the world stage, this time on Canadian soil.

LOOK OUT FOR

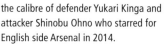

AZUSA IWASHIMIZU
Born: 14 October 1986
Position: Defender

Comfortable in possession, brave and strong. Made her debut for the senior team in 2006 and went on to feature in the FIFA Women's World Cup in 2007 and 2011. Sent off in the last minute as Japan won the competition for the first time in 2011. Loves to go up for set-pieces and grab a goal, as does her defensive partner Saki Kumagai with whom she has a great understanding. Scored two crucial goals to see Japan to victory in the AFC Women's Asian Cup.

HOMARE SAWA
Born: 6 September 1978
Position: Midfielder

Scored five goals and set up another as she skippered Japan to a famous victory in the FIFA Women's World Cup 2011 in her fifth finals appearance. She also won the tournament's Golden Ball and Boot, and went on to be crowned FIFA Women's World Player of the Year. Super-composed and with plenty of experience, this 36-year-old veteran is a big game player who continues to play her part, competing in the final as Japan lifted their first-ever AFC Women's Asian Cup in 2014.

MANA IWABUCHI
Born: 18 March 1993
Position: Forward

This diminutive striker is a big hitter on the pitch, with a breathtaking touch and sublime skill. Arrived on the international scene as a teenager in the FIFA U-17 Women's World Cup 2008; crowned the tournament's Golden Ball and then AFC women's youth player of the year. Part of the FIFA Women's World Cup 2011 title winning side, she has gone on to work on her talent by playing in Germany and joined Bayern Munich in 2014. Great role model for any young player.

SWITZERLAND
DEBUTANTS LOOK TO MAKE AN IMPACT

Switzerland are among the debutants at this expanded FIFA Women's World Cup. They were the first European side to qualify. Will they maintain their winning ways in Canada?

COACH

MARTINA VOSS-TECKLENBURG
A former German international, 47-year-old Voss-Tecklenburg knows a thing or two about football. A veteran of three FIFA Women's World Cups and a four-time Euro winner, she was an attacking midfielder/forward with 125 caps for her country. Won a host of titles as a player with TSV Siegen. Went on to taste success as a coach when she guided FCR 2001 Duisburg to two German cups and victory in the UEFA Women's Cup 2009. Worked as editor-in-chief of German women's football magazine FF for five years. Joined Switzerland in 2012 after a brief stint with FF USV Jena and has instilled a winning mentality, overseeing an unbeaten qualifying campaign.

The Swiss would like to think so, particularly when they look back at a blistering qualification campaign. Iceland, Israel, Serbia, Malta and UEFA Women's Euro 2013 semi-finalists Denmark all had to be overcome on the road to Canada.

Switzerland made light work of these obstacles, conceding just one goal and hitting an impressive 53 past their group rivals, including 16 on aggregate against both Serbia and Malta.

Their 9–0 obliteration of Israel in June 2014, coupled with the 1–1 draw between Denmark and Iceland the following day confirmed Switzerland's qualification with two games to spare.

"No one could have expected us to go through so easily," said head coach Martina Voss-Tecklenburg after she and her squad had followed the stalemate between Denmark and Iceland on the internet with eager anticipation.

Switzerland continued to make it look easy with two further victories to conclude their campaign unbeaten and nine points clear of nearest rivals Iceland.

Of course, the Swiss surprised onlookers in the qualifiers for the 2011 edition of the FIFA Women's World Cup too; then they topped their group but missed out in that tournament's play-offs.

When coach Beatrice von Siebenthal

Switzerland cruised towards Canada in qualifying; they will be ready to kick off against Japan in Vancouver.

KEY PLAYER

RAMONA BACHMANN
Born: 25 December 1990

She has been dubbed the "Swiss Magician" and first stunned Europe in 2009 when she unveiled her bag of tricks in the UEFA European Women's Under-19 Championship. Named Golden Player of that tournament, she was also voted Swiss player of the year in 2009. A precocious talent, the 24-year-old striker is skilful and strong, and few can rival her killer touch in front of goal. Signed for Umea IK in the Swedish Damallsvenskan at the age of 16 and went on to play for Atlanta Beat in the Women's Professional Soccer league in America and Swedish champions LdB FC Malmo (now known as FC Rosengard). Voted Damallsvenskan player of the year in 2011 and 2013, the Swiss No. 10 is a definite crowd pleaser.

WOMEN'S WORLD CUP RECORD

No more play-offs or repechage disappointment for Switzerland, who made no mistakes this time around. This will be their first finals appearance.

stepped down she left a side capable of mixing it with the best in Europe and the Nati have kicked on since Voss-Tecklenburg took the reins in January 2012.

An advocate of solidity in defence while making the most of a wealth of attacking talent, the former German international is keen on creativity, courage and confidence.

The Swiss have that in spades, particularly in midfielder Lara Dickenmann and strikers Ana Maria Crnogorcevic and Ramona Bachmann, who have experience of playing league football in France, Germany and Sweden respectively.

They are not alone; several Swiss seniors make their living in competitive leagues outside their home country, on-field nous which is paying off for the national side. As is the know-how that some of Voss-Tecklenburg's squad will have picked up in both a string of FIFA U-20 Women's World Cup finals appearances and at Switzerland's national academy, which gives the best young players a chance to combine football with study.

Having finally reached a major senior tournament, the Swiss now have a chance to teach the world how far this small nation has come.

LOOK OUT FOR

NOELLE MARITZ
Born: 23 December 1995
Position: Defender

Cool, strong and pacy, 19-year-old Maritz was born in America and grew up playing football and baseball. Competed in mixed teams and can mix it with the strongest opponents. Made the first-team squad at FC Zurich aged just 15 and was signed by German giants VfL Wolfsburg in 2013. Represented Switzerland in major tournaments at youth level before making her senior debut in 2013. She featured in every Switzerland game in the qualifiers.

LIA WALTI
Born: 19 April 1993
Position: Midfielder

A former Young Boys star, this versatile player can hold her own in centre-midfield, left-wing or even left-back. A fine crosser of the ball. Played in the UEFA Women's Champions League with Young Boys and was snapped up by German Frauen-Bundesliga powerhouse 1.FFC Turbine Potsdam in 2013. Starred for Switzerland in the under-age groups before breaking into the senior team. Played a large part in the qualifying campaign for Canada and will relish her chance on the big stage.

LARA DICKENMANN
Born: 27 November 1985
Position: Midfielder

Five-time Swiss player of the year, 29-year-old Dickenmann can play through the middle or on the left, where her speed and directness can be devastatingly effective. Capable of goals that will take your breath away, she scored on her debut for the senior side aged 16. Played football in America at both college and W-League level. Joined Olympique Lyonnais in 2008 where she has won the UEFA Women's Champions League and a string of French titles.

Group C

CAMEROON

LIONESSES LOOK TO BUILD ON OLYMPIC LESSONS

Cameroon were described as a "powerhouse" side on their way to qualification for Canada 2015. Will they be too strong for the top teams to handle in Canada? The Indomitable Lionesses will certainly offer every side they encounter a tough test.

COACH

CARL ENOW NGACHU
A former footballer and physical education teacher, the experienced 40-year-old coach has worked with Cameroon's national women's teams for more than a decade, at both youth and senior levels. He has rebuilt the Indomitable Lionesses squad to create a heady mix of experience and youth. Took Cameroon to victory in the All Africa Games in 2011 and secured a place at the London 2012 Olympics. Although they fared poorly in the latter competition, he remained upbeat and optimistic about their future. His confidence was rewarded in October 2014 when Cameroon qualified for their first-ever FIFA Women's World Cup.

They will relish their chance to do so too – the Lionesses have gradually developed since their maiden competition outing 24 years ago and this is the first time they have qualified for a FIFA Women's World Cup. That is not to say that Cameroon are short on tournament experience; they have plenty on their own continent and are almost perennial semi-finalists in the African Women's Championship.

Under head coach Carl Enow Ngachu, the Lionesses have kicked on even more in recent years, however, and in 2011 Cameroon were crowned champions at the All Africa Games in Mozambique without conceding a goal. In 2012 they got the chance to impose themselves on the world when they became one of only three African sides to compete at a Women's Olympic Football Tournament. Losses in the London 2012 Olympics to hosts Great Britain as well as Brazil and New Zealand were chastening, though probably not surprising given that women's football in Cameroon is still a work in progress.

Ngachu was determined that his young and spirited side should learn from their Olympic experience, though, and they will get the chance to show the world how far they have come at Canada 2015. "We are looking forward to having an impact," Ngachu said after his group had qualified

These tough cookies from Cameroon will relish the chance to compete against two fellow debutants.

KEY PLAYER

GAELLE ENGANAMOUIT
Born: 9 June 1992

Tall, strong and pacy player who is the spearhead of Cameroon's frontline. Started playing football with her brothers at the age of five and has a life-long passion for the game. Was part of Cameroon's All Africa Games winning squad in 2011, scoring in the semi-final win over South Africa. Also in the squad for the London 2012 Olympics. Played a key role in Cameroon's qualification for Canada 2015, scoring three goals and winning player of the match plaudits. Has experience of playing in Sweden's highly competitive Damallsvenskan after joining Eskilstuna United DFF from Spartak Subotica in Serbia. Has been described as one of Cameroon's precious gems because of her fine football brain, confidence under pressure and attacking ability.

WOMEN'S WORLD CUP RECORD

Cameroon's runners-up spot at the African Women's Championship ensured they continued to break new ground, earning a place at their first FIFA Women's World Cup.

for this summer's FIFA tournament by reaching the final of the African Women's Championship in October 2014.

Although favourites Nigeria went on to deny them the chance of lifting their first African Women's Championship title, Cameroon left Namibia having impressed with their strength in defence, discipline in midfield and liveliness in attack. Key to that hard-earned reputation were players such as goalkeeper of the tournament Annette Ngo Ndom, skipper Christine Manie and star striker Gaelle Enganamouit. All three boast UEFA Women's Champions League experience and they are not the only members of the group testing their talent by playing in demanding leagues outside of Africa.

Many of the current squad have played their club football in Europe and their experiences will undoubtedly help those youngsters in the group who continue to develop their game in clubs within Cameroon. These are heady days for this promising group. They have already shown their power and determination in Africa – now it is time for them to flex their footballing muscle in front of the world.

LOOK OUT FOR

ANNETTE NGO NDOM
Born: 2 June 1985
Position: Goalkeeper

Debuted for the national side in 2010 and a year later won gold at the All Africa Games in Mozambique. Hailed for her brilliance during the victory over Nigeria that booked Cameroon's qualification for the London 2012 Olympics. Has played in the UEFA Women's Champions League with Slovakian side FC Union Nove Zamky and was named best keeper in the African Women's Championship in 2014. Nominated for the 2014 African Women's Player of the Year award.

CHRISTINE MANIE
Born: 4 May 1984
Position: Defender

Composed defender who manages to pop up with crucial goals at key times: scored against Nigeria in the game that secured Cameroon's place at the London 2012 Olympics. The skipper also headed home a late-late winner in the African Women's Championship semi-final against Cote d'Ivoire to guarantee her side a place in the FIFA Women's World Cup 2015. Has UEFA Women's Champions League experience with Romanian outfit Olimpia Cluj Napoca.

MADELEINE NGONO MANI
Born: 16 October 1983
Position: Forward

The side's speedy and super-efficient goal machine and one of Cameroon's most popular players ever, she first came to prominence with Cameroonian clubs Lorema and Canon Yaounde. Has played for several teams in France including Saint-Etienne, ASJ Soyaux and Guingamp. Has a raft of tournament experience and scored the winning goal for Cameroon when they won the 2011 All Africa Games. Played every match of their historic qualification campaign for the FIFA Women's World Cup 2015.

ECUADOR

LA TRICOLOR EMBARK ON THEIR NEXT BIG ADVENTURE

When Ecuador learnt of their opponents in the FIFA Women's World Cup 2015, their coach declared that they were set to experience an "amazing adventure". That much is true, although their journey to get there was pretty incredible too.

COACH

VANESSA ARAUZ

The youngest coach in the history of any FIFA World Women's Cup tournament, Arauz will be just 26 when she leads La Tri at Canada 2015. Having joined Club Sport Emelec as a child she went on to play for a regional select XI before becoming the first woman in Ecuador to qualify as a top level coach. A dedicated scholar of the game she undertook internships with professional men's clubs before joining La Tri as an assistant coach in 2011. Stepped up to the main coaching role with the national team, as well as the youth squads, in March 2013.

That is because La Tri had needed to stage a tremendous comeback to even stay in contention for FIFA Women's World Cup 2015 qualification and were then thrown into a last-gasp intercontinental play-off with Trinidad and Tobago to settle which of them would take the very last place on offer in Canada this summer.

Two automatic qualifying places and one intercontinental play-off berth for Canada 2015 were on offer at the Copa America Femenina in September 2014 and after beating Peru and Venezuela in their group phase matches, hosts Ecuador joined Brazil, Colombia and Argentina in the battle to clinch one of those spots.

A humbling 4–0 loss to As Canarinhas and 2–1 defeat at the hands of Las Cafeteras meant Ecuador needed to beat Argentina to finish third and reach the play-offs, but their dream looked in tatters when Las Albicelestes hit them with two early goals at Atahualpa Olympic Stadium in Quito. Ecuador were not finished, though, and they turned their motivational motto "Nothing will stop us" into reality, rallying to turn around the tie and clinch the match 3–2. Their reward was another high pressure game at the same venue a month later against Trinidad and Tobago, who had finished fourth in their own continental qualifiers.

Strong-willed and able, the newcomers from Ecuador could spring a surprise.

KEY PLAYER

ANDREA PESANTES
Born: 14 January 1988

A determined and energetic all-rounder (she also enjoys swimming, athletics and cycling) who was born in the Galapagos Islands. Played in defence and midfield when younger but is now the lynchpin around whom Ecuador build their attacks. Has excellent close control and protects the ball well, especially in tight spaces, and has the confidence, energy and technical ability to inspire her team-mates in crucial matches. She represented her country at the South American Under-19 Women's Championship in 2004, aged just 16, and went on to play in Ecuador's first appearance at the Pan American Games. In 2013, she played in the inaugural season of the Ecuadorian national women's championship and won the title with Rocafuerte FC in 2014.

WOMEN'S WORLD CUP RECORD

Ecuador were the last team to qualify for the finals – their debut at the competition – after defeating Trinidad and Tobago in an intercontinental play-off.

Neither side made the breakthrough in that first leg, the game finishing goalless, so it was all to play for on 2 December in the return in Port of Spain. It was Ecuador's first away match of their entire qualifying trail and, spurred on by their "12th Warrior" fans at the Hasely Crawford Stadium, Trinidad and Tobago tested the visitors' defensive line time and again. The breakthrough, when it came, though, was Ecuador's and the late-late winner from Monica Quinteros was a historic moment for her country.

Women's football is still developing in Ecuador, but a new league is in place and several members of the national side train every day with the 2014 champions Rocafuerte FC; a handful have even enjoyed silver medal success in the Bolivarian Games in 2009.

As they showed in their thrilling qualifying campaign, Ecuador are adaptable and determined. If they can show the same fight and ambition in Canada, we will all enjoy their next great adventure.

LOOK OUT FOR

SHIRLEY BERRUZ
Born: 6 January 1991
Position: Goalkeeper

A keeper with great agility and quick reflexes who was hailed as one of the heroines of La Tri's qualification for Canada after her raft of reaction stops in the play-off against Trinidad and Tobago. Having first tried football in her mid-teens she was starting in goal for Ecuador before she hit 20. Received a pair of gloves from her hero, former national team goalkeeper Marcelo Elizaga, and was inspired to train even harder – dedication that is certainly paying off now.

LIGIA MOREIRA
Born: 19 March 1992
Position: Defender

Has captained her club side and first wore the armband for La Tri in the lead-up to the Copa America Femenina – given the honour by coach Arauz thanks to her strong character and leadership qualities at centre-back as well as her calmness in possession and good distribution. Known as "Gigi" to her team mates, she first played football as a midfielder in a boys' team. A multiple title winner with Rocafuerte, she has also played in the Copa Libertadores Femenina.

MONICA QUINTEROS
Born: 5 July 1988
Position: Forward

Monica Quinteros wrote her name into the history books after heading the goal in time added on away to Trinidad and Tobago that saw her team qualify for their first ever FIFA Women's World Cup. A quick and powerful striker, in 2014 the former Ecuador under-19 international hit 25 goals for Club 7 de Febrero. Missed the main qualifying tournament, the Copa America Femenina, on home soil due to her physical education teaching commitments.

Opened in 2013, the stadium in Winnipeg is the newest of the venues for the FIFA Women's World Cup 2015.

GROUP D

There is no doubt that the D in this group is for death! This is the fifth time Sweden and USA have been drawn together at this stage and the Americans have the edge with three wins. With Nigeria and Australia completing the line-up, fans are in for a treat.

Group D

USA

TEAM USA CROSS THE BORDER AS MAJOR CONTENDERS

Two-time FIFA Women's World Cup winners and losing finalists in the last edition of the competition, the USA are always strong favourites for the title. When they arrive in Canada, those expectations will be as high as ever.

COACH

JILL ELLIS

Former college player who took the reins in the Spring of 2014 following Tom Sermanni's departure. Has a long association with the national set-up since being appointed to lead the under-21s in 2000 by then head coach April Heinrichs. Tasted gold medal success while assistant to former USA coach Pia Sundhage at the 2008 and 2012 Olympics. Followed her father John into coaching and kicked off her own career with college sides including the UCLA Bruins, whom she led to a raft of titles. The 48-year-old is said to have coached nearly every player in the USA team pool at some stage – she knows their myriad strengths – and will relish the challenges ahead.

That is not simply because the USA have always reached at least the semi-final stage of the elite world tournament; it is also because of the prowess they showed on the road to this 2015 edition.

The USA brushed aside all-comers in the qualifying CONCACAF Women's Championship in October 2014, easing past Mexico 3–0 in the semi-final to book their place in Canada, before battering Costa Rica 6–0 in the final to win the trophy. That result brought their goal tally in the tournament to 21 without reply, an imperious vein of form made all the more impressive by the fact that new head coach Jill Ellis frequently switched around her starting XI and their positions.

Only midfielder and eventual Golden Ball winner Carli Lloyd played all 450 minutes of the competition, but the fact that Ellis was still able to get the best out of every player illustrates both her qualities as a communicator and the determination of those on her roster to perform.

From centre-back and captain Christie Rampone, down to tricky players like Tobin Heath and Megan Rapinoe, and the world's leading goalscorer Abby Wambach, these are ominous opponents for any world side to encounter. And regardless of which players make the final squad this summer, the majority will enter this

Team USA are all smiles. They are ready to do their thing ... and their thing is winning.

KEY PLAYER

ALEX MORGAN
Born: 2 July 1989

Hard-working, highly competitive and speedy striker with a clinical eye for goal, who really proved her world-class credentials in 2012 when she netted 14 goals in 12 internationals. Suffered cruciate ligament injury aged 17 but returned to impress and scored the tournament-winning goal at the FIFA U-20 Women's World Cup 2008 in Chile. Won the Women's Professional Soccer championship with Western New York Flash in 2011 and Olympic gold with the USA in 2012. She was the youngest player on the roster in the FIFA Women's World Cup 2011 and scored in the final against Japan, but had to settle for a runners-up medal. She suffered an ankle injury in the Canada 2015 qualifying campaign but when fit is the established spearhead of arguably the world's most dangerous offensive line.

WOMEN'S WORLD CUP RECORD

Year	Venue	Result
1991	China	Winners
1995	Sweden	Third place
1999	USA	Winners
2003	USA	Third place
2007	China	Third place
2011	Germany	Runners-up

FIFA Women's World Cup with painful memories of having lost in the final four years ago.

That year Japan's Nadeshiko broke USA hearts when they held their collective nerve to win the penalty shoot-out that denied the Americans a first FIFA Women's World Cup title since 1999.

English-born Ellis will lead the USA team into the tournament this time around and she knows that her job is to bring the trophy home. She will tackle the task positively – she has already stated a desire to build on the style of her predecessor Pia Sundhage – and her deployment of an attacking 4–3–3 formation in the CONCACAF Women's Championship bodes well for Canada 2015.

Skipper Rampone is the only USA player to possess a FIFA Women's World Cup-winner's medal; as they embark on a seventh consecutive appearance in the tournament, this current crop know that nothing but an outright victory will do.

LOOK OUT FOR

CHRISTIE RAMPONE
Born: 24 June 1975
Position: Defender

Inspirational and reliable captain, in 2014 this mother-of-two became only the second player ever to make 300 international appearances, the first to do so being world-record cap holder and USA legend Kristine Lilly. Made her national team debut in 1997 and was part of the USA's FIFA Women's World Cup 1999 winning squad and has gone on to collect three Olympic gold medals. Steered Sky Blue FC to the Women's Professional Soccer championship as a player-caretaker manager in 2009.

LAUREN HOLIDAY
Born: 30 September 1987
Position: Midfielder

Classy player who conducts the team from midfield with her visionary passes. Played with boys' teams until the age of 12. Part of the USA's FIFA U-20 Women's World Championship 2006 squad that came fourth and made her senior debut in 2007. Made an impact in the FIFA Women's World Cup 2011 with two goals and a place in the All-star squad after winning praise for her clinical finishing, passing and dead-ball ability. Changed her surname from Cheney after marrying NBA favourite Jrue Holiday in 2013.

MEGAN RAPINOE
Born: 5 July 1985
Position: Midfielder/Forward

Scored direct from a corner kick at the London 2012 Olympics semi-final and has the instinct and ability to light up a game. Part of the USA side that finished third in the FIFA U-19 Women's World Championship in 2004. Tore her cruciate ligament in 2006 and 2007 but made it back and was a key player as the USA finished runners-up in the senior edition in 2011. Gained experience of European football at Olympique Lyonnais in France in 2013 while on loan from her parent club Seattle Reign FC.

AUSTRALIA

MATILDAS READY TO PRESS FOR SUCCESS

Expectations are high as Australia make their sixth finals appearance at the FIFA Women's World Cup. The Matildas have reached the quarters on the last two occasions – can they raise their game further this time?

COACH

ALEN STAJCIC

Stepped in as interim coach to guide Australia through their crucial FIFA Women's World Cup qualifying competition after the departure of former boss Hesterine de Reus. Hit the ground running to book a berth in Canada and took over as permanent head coach in September 2014. Played for teams in the New South Wales Premier League and attained his coaching badges in his 20s, going on to lead successful W-League side Sydney FC. The 41-year-old is well respected in the women's game Down Under, having coached at the NSW Institute of Sport and with Sydney FC, and believes in positive, attack-minded football of the kind to excite any World Cup fan.

There is no reason why not given the dynamic crop of players who ensured that the Matildas qualified for 2015 with relatively little fuss.

Australia needed to finish in the top five at the AFC Women's Asian Cup in Vietnam in May 2014 to book a berth at this year's FIFA tournament. They arrived in Ho Chi Minh City in a state of managerial flux with an interim head coach in Alen Stajcic – but they answered his call for positive, possession football to finish as group runners-up and qualify for Canada.

Of course, there was even more at stake for the Matildas in Vietnam; Australia's women became part of the Asian confederation in 2006 and had made history when they won the AFC Women's

Asian Cup in 2010. They were eager to retain their title and a 2–1 semi-final win over ever-improving Korea Republic gave them the springboard to do so – but then they needed to overcome FIFA Women's World Cup holders Japan in the final.

Having already drawn 2–2 with the Nadeshiko in the group stages – a game Australia let slip after storming into a two-goal lead – the Matildas went into the showpiece match determined to play a pressing game.

Blessed with youth and experience, an attack-minded Matildas side pushed Japan

Will the talented Matildas come of age and waltz out of their "group of death"?

KEY PLAYER

KATE GILL
Born: 10 December 1984

This prolific striker only made her debut for the Matildas in 2004 (against the nation of her birth, New Zealand, in the Australia Cup). Yet by 2014 she had already beaten the legendary Cheryl Salisbury's 38-goal strike record to become the nation's leading scorer. Tall and skilful, she is a veteran of the FIFA Women's World Cup 2007 but missed out on the 2011 edition through injury – so will be desperate to show her prowess in 2015. Won the AFC Women's Asian Cup with Australia in 2010 and was named best female player in Asia. Joined Perth Glory FC in 2009 and went on to top-score her way to the W-League Golden Boot gong in 2013. Has gained valuable experience in recent years by playing stints in Sweden's high-octane Damallsvenskan.

WOMEN'S WORLD CUP RECORD

Year	Venue	Result
1991	China	Did not qualify
1995	Sweden	Group stage (4th, Group C)
1999	USA	Group stage (3rd, Group D)
2003	USA	Group stage (4th, Group D)
2007	China	Quarter-finalists
2011	Germany	Quarter-finalists

all the way but their title was lost thanks to a single goal from Azusa Iwashimizu.

Looking ahead, however, there is still great cause for optimism for the team from Down Under as they face an even keener test in Canada.

Since showing their elite potential with a first-ever win in the FIFA Women's World Cup at the 2007 edition, the women in green and gold have twice reached the last eight.

In 2011 they did so having had to bed-in up-and-coming youngsters following the retirements of key players in the run-up to the competition. The bulk of that 2011 squad continue to feature for a national side that is now even more experienced thanks to Australia's increasingly competitive W-League.

Leading Australia into this exciting next stage, the now-permanent Stajcic hopes his group can further develop their consistency, maturity and tactical nous.

Given past achievements, his charges will surely work their socks off to make that happen.

LOOK OUT FOR

CAITLIN FOORD
Born: 11 November 1994
Position: Defender/Midfielder

Only 16 when she ran out for Australia in the FIFA Women's World Cup 2011, Foord made such an impact in Germany as an overlapping full-back that she went on to be named best young player of the tournament. This versatile 20-year-old is classed as one of Australia's most exciting players ever. She has W-League experience with Sydney FC and Perth Glory, and has played for Sky Blue in the US National Women's Soccer League.

CLARE POLKINGHORNE
Born: 1 February 1989
Position: Defender

The 2010 Australian female footballer of the year and W-League player of the year in 2013 is a veteran of the Matildas' last two FIFA Women's World Cups. Confident and capable leader, dangerous at set-pieces, she has skippered W-League side Brisbane Roar and co-captains the Matildas with Kate Gill. Part of the 2010 AFC Women's Asian Cup winning side. She gained experience in the Japanese Nadeshiko League in 2014, playing for INAC Kobe Leonessa.

LISA DE VANNA
Born: 14 November 1984
Position: Forward

A star for the Matildas in the FIFA Women's World Cup 2007 after bagging four goals, De Vanna still has that wow factor going into 2015. Crowned Australia footballer of the year in 2013 when a wonder goal saw her shortlisted for the FIFA Puskas Award. A lively character, capable of unlocking any defence with her determination and explosive burst of pace, she is one of the Matildas' leading scorers and has played in Australia, Europe and America.

SWEDEN

SWEDES SET THEIR SIGHTS ON SILVERWARE

Sweden have finished second and third in previous editions of the FIFA Women's World Cup. After qualifying for 2015, the Blagult have set their sights on becoming medal-winners once again.

COACH

PIA SUNDHAGE

One of the game's most successful figures, as a player she won numerous Swedish league and cup titles. Capped 146 times – the first coming when she was 15 – she scored 71 goals and won European gold in 1984 and bronze in the FIFA Women's World Cup 1991. Coached Sweden's youth teams and became assistant at Philadelphia Charge in the US Women's United Soccer Association in 2001. Went on to coach Boston Breakers to the regular season title and was assistant to China PR coach Marika Domanski Lyfors in the FIFA Women's World Cup 2007. In five years as USA head coach she won FIFA Women's World Cup silver and two Olympic golds. Joined Sweden in 2012. A music lover, she was given a guitar as a leaving gift by the USA players and has been known to light up press conferences by bursting into song.

Tough and technical, the Swedes were definitely on winning form in qualification and they went into their final group match in September 2014 unbeaten. Their opponents in the deciding qualifier, however, were second-placed Scotland and there was little margin for error – the Blagult needed to avoid a 3–1 loss or worse to steer clear of the play-offs. Pia Sundhage's side duly delivered a 2–0 win, Therese Sjogran and Lotta Schelin both scoring against the Scots in front of a rapturous crowd and their "Camp Sweden" fans in Gothenburg.

That Sjogran and Schelin's goals had booked Sweden's place in the 2015 finals was fitting: the former was making her 199th appearance while the latter had equalled the scoring record of 72 set by the legendary Hanna Ljungberg. Not that those achievements were uppermost in their minds: "Priority number one was securing the World Cup spot," said Schelin. "A medal is absolutely what we are going for now."

Going for it is something Sweden have done consistently since Sundhage's penalty kick secured the first-ever European women's title in 1984. Runners-up spots in the 1987, 1995 and 2001 UEFA Women's Euros and the FIFA Women's World Cup 2003 all followed.

Yet gold continues to elude the Swedes in the modern era and in 2013 they were

This Swedish team may be in a tough group but when it comes to the big tournaments, they are always contenders.

KEY PLAYER

LOTTA SCHELIN
Born: 27 February 1984

Tall, fast and stylish, she is a clever and unselfish team player – and Sweden's all-time top striker too. Outscored her team-mates in qualification, with 12 goals in 10 appearances. Won the Golden Boot in the UEFA Women's Euro 2013 and was named in the All-star squad. Since making her debut against France in 2004, the 31-year-old has gone on to play in eight major international tournaments and was in the All-star team of the FIFA Women's World Cup 2011. Has won the UEFA Women's Champions League and numerous league titles with Olympique Lyonnais. Multiple winner of the Swedish Football Association's Diamond Ball for the nation's foremost player and crowned best female player in the country in 2013 by the French players' union.

WOMEN'S WORLD CUP RECORD

Year	Venue	Result
1991	China	Third place
1995	Sweden	Quarter-finalists
1999	USA	Quarter-finalists
2003	USA	Runners-up
2007	China	Group stage (3rd, Group B)
2011	Germany	Third place

sorely disappointed to lose to Germany in the UEFA Women's Euro semi-finals on home soil. Afterwards Sundhage said Sweden would have to go from "good to better" if they were to challenge for that elusive FIFA Women's World Cup crown in 2015 in Canada.

Going into the qualifiers, the coach kept faith with the majority of her Euro squad and she was rewarded with a string of solid wins during which they conceded just one goal. Those victories were punctuated by a mixed bag of results that included a 1–0 win over the USA in the Algarve Cup but a 2–1 loss to Iceland in the play-off for third place, and then a 4–0 friendly loss to England in August 2014.

But when Sweden faced Scotland in the crucial qualifying match for Canada, Sundhage felt her insistence on possession football concentrated in the middle of the park had finally clicked. She declared: "The players have accepted the system and we'll only keep improving from here."

LOOK OUT FOR

NILLA FISCHER
Born: 2 August 1984
Position: Defender

Switched from midfield to central defence by Sundhage, she has taken to the role so well she was named defender of the year in 2013 by the Swedish FA. Great in the air and with fine technical ability, she is another 30-something with well over 100 caps for her country. Made the All-star squad of the UEFA Women's Euro 2013 and just missed out on the 2014 UEFA European player of the year gong. Has won the UEFA Women's Champions League with VfL Wolfsburg.

ELIN RUBENSSON
Born: 11 May 1993
Position: Defender

Shone in the 2012 UEFA European Women's Under-19 Championship, top-scoring to guide Sweden to victory and earning a reputation as a big game player in the process. Named breakthrough player of 2012 by the Swedish FA. Made her debut for Sweden's seniors in October 2012. Versatile, quick and dependable, she has played at left-back, midfield and in attack. Four-time Damallsvenskan title winner with LdB FC Malmo, now known as FC Rosengard.

CAROLINE SEGER
Born: 19 March 1985
Position: Midfielder

A hard-working leader who is so influential that Sundhage changed the Swedish system to "get the most" out of her. Certainly played her part in qualifying, scoring five in nine matches. Joined Paris Saint-Germain in 2014 and has played in the US Women's Professional Soccer league, skippering Western New York Flash to the title in 2011. A veteran of many elite international tournaments, she shares the Sweden captaincy with Schelin.

NIGERIA

AFRICAN CHAMPIONS ARE NOT TO BE UNDERESTIMATED

Nigeria have qualified for every edition of the FIFA Women's World Cup finals. No elite opponent would dare dream of taking the Super Falcons lightly, but how high can this nation fly in 2015?

COACH

EDWIN OKON

Coached the Falconets to a creditable fourth-place finish in the FIFA U-20 Women's World Cup in 2012 and was asked to take over as caretaker of the senior side in 2013 after having been an assistant previously. Oversaw the return of the African Women's Championship title to Nigeria in 2014 and with it qualification for the nation's seventh successive FIFA Women's World Cup, maintaining their status as the only African side to have featured in every edition. Successful coach of Nigerian club Rivers Angels, he believes in teamwork and is unafraid to mix experience and youth in the quest for success.

The last time Nigeria really shone on the main world stage was in 1999 when they put on a stunning display in a quarter-final encounter with Brazil, coming back from 3–0 down only to lose 4–3 to Sissi's golden goal in extra time.

That finish remains Nigeria's best at any senior FIFA Women's World Cup but in every edition that has followed, they have declared a determination to better that record.

They have not gone beyond the group stages since. In 2011 they were stymied by a difficult draw that pitted them against giants of the game Germany and France. They headed home with their pride intact after losing by a single goal to both those opponents while beating Canada 1–0 with a squad that featured a host of players with experience of FIFA U-17 and U-20 Women's World Cups.

Under new boss Edwin Okon that emphasis on youth continues and the squad has been rebuilt since faring poorly in the African Women's Championship in 2012. In October 2014 when they regained their title, they did so with a physically strong and athletic 21-woman squad that ranged in age from 17 to 38.

Stars such as Sweden-based Perpetua Nkwocha, four-time FIFA Women's World Cup veteran Stella Mbachu and goalkeeper

Strong and athletic are always words used to describe Nigeria; with this line-up, you can add exciting to the list.

KEY PLAYER

ASISAT OSHOALA
Born: 9 October 1994

The Super Falcons may well have found a successor to their star player Perpetua Nkwocha in this talented and versatile youngster. Capable of spectacular goals, she stood out in the FIFA U-20 Women's World Cup 2014 in Canada, where she won the Golden Boot and Ball after scoring seven goals and winning three player of the match awards. Was awarded a national honour by Nigerian president Goodluck Jonathan after the tournament. Only just turned 20 when Nigeria lifted their seventh African Women's Championship title in October 2014, she was named the most valuable player of the tournament. Thought to be on the wish list of several European clubs, she rounded off the year by winning both African women's player and youth player of the year.

WOMEN'S WORLD CUP RECORD

Year	Venue	Result
1991	China	Group stage (4th, Group C)
1995	Sweden	Group stage (4th, Group B)
1999	USA	Quarter-finalists
2003	USA	Group stage (4th, Group A)
2007	China	Group stage (4th, Group B)
2011	Germany	Group stage (3rd, Group A)

Precious Dede returned to bring their vast experience to the side.

But 11 of the players that clinched the hard-fought 2–0 victory over Cameroon which secured a record seventh African Women's Championship title for Nigeria were aged 23-and-under.

Okon insists there are no stars in this Nigeria squad, and his teams were solid from front to back throughout the tournament in Namibia. But two of his promising youngsters eclipsed the opposition to receive honours at the tournament's close, with France-based forward Desire Oparanozie top-scoring, while FIFA U-20 Women's World Cup 2014 starlet Asisat Oshoala was named most valuable player.

Such a wealth of young talent suggests that Nigeria will continue to be a nation to watch when the FIFA Women's World Cup kicks off.

And if they receive the support enjoyed by other elite sides, Nigeria will go from strength to strength.

LOOK OUT FOR

NGOZI EBERE
Born: 5 August 1991
Position: Defender

Hard-working and forceful left-back who likes to get forward and take responsibility for set-pieces. Has progressed from the under-20s to the senior set-up and put on a player-of-the-match performance in the 2014 African Women's Championship, setting up two goals and impressing technical experts with her work rate. A key defender for Nigeria in the qualification tournament, this determined player will be difficult to beat in Canada.

EVELYN NWABUOKU
Born: 14 November 1985
Position: Defender/Midfielder

The Super Falcons' versatile skipper is a reassuring presence on the pitch where she leads by example with her coolness under pressure, quick feet and incisive passing. She experienced the FIFA U-19 Women's World Championship 2004 and has gone on to become an integral member of the senior side, more than playing her part in the Super Falcons' qualification for Canada 2015. Has led Nigerian Women's Premier League side Rivers Angels to domestic honours.

DESIRE OPARANOZIE
Born: 17 December 1993
Position: Forward

Tenacious and powerful, she made her mark in the FIFA U-17 and U-20 Women's World Cups and was a key figure for the under-20 Falconets in 2010 when Nigeria went all the way to a final match-up against eventual winners Germany; ever-present when they finished fourth in 2012. Started all three games in the senior 2011 edition, including the 1–0 win over Canada. Has European experience with FC Rossiyanka of Russia and Guingamp in France.

The Olympic Stadium in Montreal is the largest venue at the FIFA Women's World Cup 2015.

GROUP E

With ever-present finals nation Brazil playing a more competitive Korea Republic side than the one they dismissed by three goals without reply in 2003, and the intriguing prospect of Spain taking on fellow debutants Costa Rica, recording a solid opening result could be key to this finely poised group.

BRAZIL

CAN THE YELLOW JERSEYS OF BRAZIL LIGHT UP CANADA 2015?

Brazil are the only side from South America to have reached every edition of the FIFA Women's World Cup. The naturally talented As Canarinhas players came within a whisper of gold in 2007 – how will this group fare in 2015?

COACH

OSWALDO ALVAREZ

Known as Vadao, the experienced 58-year-old is renowned for his work in men's football, having coached in Brazil's Serie A, B and C at clubs including Corinthians and Sao Paulo. Boasts a reputation as a student of the game and is also known for his ability to bring through young players – is said to have discovered world-class stars such as Rivaldo and Kaka. Tactically and defensively astute while also being attack-minded. Took over the women's national side in 2014 and has described it as one of his biggest challenges yet. Negotiated the first hurdle by ensuring that Brazil reached Canada 2015.

Certainly Brazil shone brightly enough in the Copa America Femenina competition that decided which two of 10 South American sides would directly make it to the 2015 edition. Despite heading to Ecuador in September 2014 without star striker Marta in the squad, Oswaldo Alvarez's players bossed the championship, losing just one match of seven in 17 intense days of football.

Veteran forward Cristiane, 37-year-old keeper Andreia and exciting youngsters such as defender Tayla stepped up to the plate as the challenges of Bolivia, Paraguay, Chile and Ecuador were all comfortably dismissed.

A 2–0 defeat by Argentina in the group phase was the only downside of the tournament, although that largely reserve team loss was avenged with a comprehensive 6–0 victory over Las Albicelestes in the final phase.

Colombia proved more stubborn opponents in the last match, but the resulting 0–0 draw between the two was enough for both nations to qualify for Canada 2015. "It's been a brilliant campaign," said Vadao afterwards.

Indeed it was, given that Brazil had not only qualified for the FIFA Women's World Cup, they had claimed a sixth South American Championship title too. Such

Brazil are always full of flair and with Rio 2016 on the horizon, this side might be more prepared than any of their predecessors.

KEY PLAYER

MARTA
Born: 19 February 1986

What more can be said about the five-time FIFA Women's World Player of the Year that has not been said before? One of the world's best-known female players, she possesses unparalleled speed on the ball. First lit up the world stage in the FIFA U-19 Women's World Championship 2002, winning the Silver Ball before going on to claim the Golden Ball in the 2004 edition. Won Olympic silver that year too – but really came to the fore in the FIFA Women's World Cup 2007 in China when she scored seven goals and ran off with the Golden Shoe and Golden Ball gongs. Currently shares the top all-time FIFA Women's World Cup goalscorer record with Birgit Prinz. Has won multiple titles with clubs in Sweden and America.

WOMEN'S WORLD CUP RECORD

Year	Venue	Result
1991	China	Group stage (3rd, Group B)
1995	Sweden	Group stage (4th, Group A)
1999	USA	Third place
2003	USA	Quarter-finalists
2007	China	Runners-up
2011	Germany	Quarter-finalists

domination of their own confederation has yet to be repeated on the world stage, however.

Since their breakthrough in 1999, they have always reached the quarter-finals of the FIFA Women's World Cup but have yet to better 2007's showing of second.

And while their Olympic record is even more impressive, with two silver medals and two fourth-place finishes achieved, their failure to progress beyond the quarter-finals at the London 2012 Olympics was disappointing to say the least.

Since then, though, more regular participation in friendlies as well as their own annual invitational tournament ought to present its gifted individuals with the opportunity to develop together as a smart unit and gel as a formidable squad.

Striving for that cohesion is particularly vital when so many players have departed abroad in search of improved playing opportunities. Given the ever-shrinking margins for error at the elite level, tactical understanding and the ability to react and adapt to changing situations is key. For As Canarinhas this summer, it might just be the difference between promising and delivering.

LOOK OUT FOR

FORMIGA
Born: 3 March 1978
Position: Midfielder

A ball-winning defensive midfielder of the highest order, the 37-year-old has earned the respect of her peers at the elite level and is a symbol of the women's game in Brazil. Has represented her country in every FIFA Women's World Cup since 1995 and is the only player to have appeared at every Olympics since 1996. Has turned out for several clubs in Brazil as well as Malmo FF in Sweden and New Jersey Wildcats, FC Gold Pride and Chicago Red Stars in America.

CRISTIANE
Born: 15 May 1985
Position: Forward

This punchy, intelligent and powerful striker came through the youth ranks alongside Marta with whom she has enjoyed a deadly partnership over the years. Scored the fastest hat-trick in the women's Olympics in 2008 and was the competition's top scorer. Has twice come third in the FIFA Women's World Player of the Year awards and experts described her as "exceptional" in the FIFA Women's World Cup 2007. Has masses of experience, having played in Brazil, Europe and America.

ANDRESSA
Born: 1 May 1995
Position: Forward

Gifted player, also known as Andressinha, who is seen by many in Brazil as the closest to Marta when it comes to natural talent. Plays with flair as well as passion and excelled at youth level in the creative No. 10 role. Has been labelled "captain extraordinaire" for her performances in youth championships in South America and has also appeared for Brazil in FIFA U-17 and U-20 Women's World Cups, earning praise for her ability to read the game.

KOREA REPUBLIC
TALENTED TAEGUK LADIES AIM HIGH

Korea Republic could well be one of the dark horses of the FIFA Women's World Cup 2015. They debuted in the 2003 tournament but did not win a game and had not qualified since – until now. A challenge awaits; can they rise to it?

COACH

YOON DEOK-YEO

Having represented his country as a player, this coach knows how it feels to play on the biggest stage of all. The 54-year-old former defender, who expects his sides to defend well too, played for Korea Republic during their first-round exit at the 1990 FIFA World Cup. Experience garnered as a player in the domestic K-League has not been lost – he turned to coaching. Several K-League clubs and the Korea Republic boys' team that played in the FIFA U-17 World Championship in 2003 have all benefited from his expertise. Joined the women's side in 2013 and oversaw a high-scoring qualification campaign.

If gifted playmaker Ji So-yun is a yardstick for the level of talent available to coach Yoon Deok-yeo then they may well do. Blessed with superb vision and even better ball control, Ji lit up the FA Women's Super League in England in 2014 and she is desperate for her team to do the same in Canada this summer.

"Of course our aim is to win," she said. "I believe if you are a football player, you must always aim high and play to win the World Cup."

The Taeguk Ladies disappointed in the 2003 edition but the Korea Republic we can expect to see in 2015 are well equipped for tournament play. A host of players have gained experience at FIFA under-age championships and they are quick and tidy footballers boasting great technique and a hard edge.

Ji's strike partner Yeo Min-ji and dynamic midfielder Lee So-dam were FIFA U-17 Women's World Cup winners in 2010 and they, and several of that year's bronze-winning FIFA U-20 Women's World Cup side, are now involved in the senior set-up.

Complementing these rising stars of Asian football are veterans such as Park Eun-sun, who top-scored as Korea Republic qualified for the FIFA Women's World Cup 2015 via the AFC Women's Asian Cup.

Coach Yoon Deok-yeo's squad needed

Many of the Taeguk Ladies, pictured here at the 2014 Asian Games, have won medals at youth level.

KEY PLAYER

JI SO-YUN
Born: 21 February 1991

Anyone who witnessed the four-time Korean player of the year play for Chelsea Ladies in the English FA Women's Super League in 2014 will know that she is something special. Small and compact, Ji has the ability to baffle defenders with her dribbling skills but she is no showboater – she can score and bring other players into the game too. Ideally likes to play in the No. 10 role but, as her displays for Chelsea proved, she is flexible and willing to play anywhere across the forward line or in midfield. Ji made her debut for Korea at the tender age of 15 and went on to play in Japan for INAC Kobe Leonessa. She signed a two-year deal with Chelsea in January 2014 and was named FA WSL Players' Player of the Year in her first season.

WOMEN'S WORLD CUP RECORD

Year	Venue	Result
1991	China	Did not qualify
1995	Sweden	Did not qualify
1999	USA	Did not qualify
2003	USA	Group stage (4th, Group B)
2007	China	Did not qualify
2011	Germany	Did not qualify

to be one of the top five teams in the competition in Vietnam in May 2014 to book a spot in Canada and Park bossed the scoring charts as the Koreans obliterated Mynamar 12–0 and beat fellow 2015 qualifiers Thailand 4–0.

Those results were enough to see them through to Canada and they concluded their group with a goalless draw against China PR.

Park's second-half penalty kept her side in the semi-final against Australia that followed but the Koreans were overcome 2–1 in Ho Chi Minh City.

If that was a bitter pill, the loss to China by a late-late goal in the battle for third place in Thong Nhat Stadium was even harder to swallow.

Yet while Yoon felt their physicality was lacking against the Matildas, he was pleased with his charges and expects them to push on when they reach the ultimate world stage.

LOOK OUT FOR

LEE SO-DAM
Born: 12 October 1994
Position: Midfielder

Already a veteran of three under-age FIFA Women's World Cups, this lively midfielder is energetic and confident. Blessed with great balance – she is a natural at Taekwondo too – she also has great positional awareness. Loves to supply pin-point crosses and free-kicks and puts in the hours on the training pitch to get them inch-perfect. Small in stature, she's a big game player nonetheless, scoring in the final to help her country lift the FIFA U-17 Women's World Cup in 2010.

PARK EUN-SUN
Born: 25 December 1986
Position: Forward

It is 12 years since striker Park first lit up the international scene. Tall and strong, she played every one of Korea's FIFA Women's World Cup 2003 games and she was only 16. She has since said the competition came too soon for her – but she is ready for 2015. Park left Korea for Russian side FC Rossiyanka and, despite a long hiatus from international football, she can still produce at the elite level – as her goals in the 2014 AFC Women's Asian Cup showed.

YEO MIN-JI
Born: 27 April 1993
Position: Forward

Yeo enjoyed a breakthrough international season in 2010, winning the FIFA U-17 Women's World Cup, the tournament's Golden Ball and Boot and the AFC women's youth player of the year gong. A determined goal-getter, she can have fans up on their feet in appreciation of her mazy runs. And run she can, with a great engine, plus balance and poise. Yeo has developed a great understanding with Ji So-yun and is definitely one to watch.

SPAIN

LA ROJA LOOK TO BUILD ON HISTORIC DEBUT

Spain have never qualified for the FIFA Women's World Cup before now but with a rising reputation it was only a matter of time before they did. So how far will these debutants go?

COACH

IGNACIO QUEREDA

"Nacho" has led the women's side since 1988. The 64-year-old played on the wing for Real Madrid's youth team and coached men's side CD Mostoles in Spain's third division before teaming up with the women's national squad. Led Spain's 2004 UEFA European Women's Under-19 Championship-winning side and took the seniors to an impressive quarter-final berth at the UEFA Women's Euro 2013, their first major finals in 16 years. A respected technician of the game, he has brought through several youth players into the senior set-up and enjoyed the fruits of his labour when Spain qualified for the FIFA Women's World Cup 2015, their third major senior tournament under his charge.

La Roja were as successful as it was possible to be when it came to qualification for Canada, winning Group 2 with a game to go thanks to Natalia Pablos's brace in a 2–0 victory away to Romania. Estonia, FYR Macedonia, Czech Republic and tricky Italy were also dismissed on the road to Canada 2015 as Spain finished three points clear of the Azzurre, the only team to take points off them in an unbeaten campaign.

Spain's historic achievement was well met by a football-obsessed nation and they made headlines across the country. There were bravos aplenty on social media too, with Spain and Manchester United goalkeeper David de Gea sending "las chicas" his congratulations via Twitter. The plaudits were merited, given the flair with which Spain had qualified, and their European rivals quickly discovered that what La Roja lack in size they more than make up for in work rate and talent.

The squad that secured qualification featured the core of the side that had so impressed when Spain reached the last eight of the UEFA Women's Euro 2013. In the aftermath of that tournament in Sweden, Spain were noted as technically gifted by official observers who also compared them favourably to the men's national side that had recently won a hat-trick of major titles.

La Roja feel like they've been so close for so many years, now they are Canada-bound and raring to go.

KEY PLAYER

VERONICA BOQUETE
Born: 9 April 1987

With outstanding technical ability, two good feet and playmaking vision, Spain's co-captain will delight FIFA Women's World Cup audiences. Hard-working and hungry, she believes in herself and her team. Won the 2004 UEFA European Women's Under-19 Championship and was named in the All-star team of the FIFA U-19 Women's World Championship that same year. Took her senior bow in 2005 and made the All-star squad of the UEFA Women's Euro 2013. Picks up plaudits wherever she plays, most impressively in America, where she was named Michelle Akers Women's Professional Soccer league player of the year in 2011 and Portland Thorns FC supporters' player of 2014. In Sweden she was crowned midfielder of the year after winning the league with Tyreso FF in 2012. Played her football with German outfit 1. FFC Frankfurt in 2014.

WOMEN'S WORLD CUP RECORD

Conceding only two goals in their whole qualifying campaign, Spain are on their way to their first ever FIFA Women's World Cup.

High praise indeed – and Spain's slick attacks and short, sharp passing game successfully propelled them into the quarter-finals of the competition, although eventual silver medal-winners Norway won out 3–1.

Long-standing coach Ignacio Quereda maintained that Spain still needed to build their "big-match experience" when they left Scandinavia. Several of his players already have that, a handful having won gold either in the 2004 UEFA European Women's Under-19 Championship or the Under-17 Championship in 2010 and 2011. Domestically, the squad are gaining experience too. Several competed in highly competitive leagues in Europe and America in 2014, while others tasted UEFA Women's Champions League football with FC Barcelona.

The FIFA Women's World Cup will be their biggest test to date but, with the wealth of talent at their disposal, Spain will work hard to make it a debut to remember.

LOOK OUT FOR

MARTA TORREJON
Born: 27 February 1990
Position: Defender

Played football with boys until the age of 14 and is a solid central defender who leads by example. Skippered Spain in the UEFA European Women's Under-19 Championship in 2007 and 2008 and RCD Espanyol, where she won league and cup honours. Added to her trophy cabinet after joining Barcelona. Debuted for Spain's seniors in 2007 and featured in every game of the UEFA Women's Euro 2013 and all the qualifiers for Canada. Brother Marc is a professional footballer.

JENNIFER HERMOSO
Born: 9 May 1990
Position: Midfielder/Forward

Versatile attacker with a great left foot who loves to make goals as well as score them. Scored the goal that won Rayo Vallecano the Spanish title in 2011 and gained experience in the demanding Swedish Damallsvenskan with Tyreso before returning to Spain with Barcelona in 2014. Made her senior debut for Spain in 2012 and was ever-present as La Roja made the quarter-finals of the UEFA Women's Euro 2013, scoring twice. Bagged seven goals in 10 qualifiers.

NATALIA PABLOS
Born: 15 October 1985
Position: Forward

An instinctive finisher who won multiple titles with Rayo Vallecano, captaining the club and scoring over 300 goals in nearly 13 years. Left in 2013 to join Bristol Academy WFC in the English FA Women's Super League, then under current England coach Mark Sampson, and moved to Arsenal Ladies for the 2015 season. Another of Spain's 2004 UEFA European Women's Under-19 Championship victors, she scored 12 goals in 10 games in qualifying.

COSTA RICA
LAS TICAS TAKING THEIR RAPID RISE IN THEIR STRIDE

Costa Rica became the first Central American side to qualify for Canada 2015. Their achievement shows how far the women's game has advanced in this small but ambitious footballing nation – but they know that this is still a work in progress.

COACH

AMELIA VALVERDE

When then head coach Carlos Garabet Avedissian announced his departure in January 2015, one of his assistants, 28-year-old Amelia Valverde was appointed as his replacement. A central defender with first division side Flores for eight years, Valverde then served as its head coach for a further two. In 2011 she joined Costa Rica as conditioning coach, progressing to assistant with the under-20s and seniors, and head of the under-17s. She knows the players and system well and though shy away from football, she will relish the responsibility of taking her team to the world stage.

A third-place finish in 1998 was Costa Rica's previous best at a CONCACAF Women's World Cup qualifying tournament, but in 2014 they managed to finish as runners-up, losing only to the USA in the final and playing an entertaining brand of football in the process.

Along the way, Las Ticas beat Mexico for the first time ever and they bossed Trinidad and Tobago in the semi-final, although it eventually took a penalty shoot-out to settle that match in their favour and guarantee an automatic berth for the FIFA Women's World Cup 2015.

"There's nothing to do but celebrate," said Costa Rica goalkeeper Dinnia Diaz after performing heroics during the shoot-out and saving three spot-kicks. "You celebrate because we're in the World Cup. In the end, it's not just the team, but the country that celebrates this victory."

Given that Costa Ricans came out in record numbers to watch the FIFA U-17 Women's World Cup in March 2014, it does indeed look as though the nation is behind the women's game. Costa Rica president Luis Guillermo Solis reflected the mood of the country when he telephoned then head coach Carlos Garabet Avedissian to congratulate him on achieving qualification for Canada 2015.

A humbling 6–0 loss to the USA in the

Las Ticas may be out-sized by some of their opponents but they will not be out-fought.

KEY PLAYER

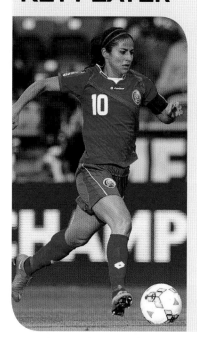

SHIRLEY CRUZ
Born: 28 August 1985

Has blazed a trail for female footballers in Costa Rica and is ahead of the curve in terms of her ability and development, so it will be great to see her feature at a FIFA Women's World Cup while still in her prime. Moved to France to join Olympique Lyonnais in 2006 on a semi-professional basis. Her terrier-like work-rate and technical excellence earned her a two-year professional contract with the French champions in 2009 and she was part of the all-conquering side that went on to win the UEFA Women's Champions League two years in a row. Became a regular starter for Paris Saint-Germain after signing for Lyon's rivals in 2012. She was named the best female player in France by the French Football Federation in 2013.

WOMEN'S WORLD CUP RECORD

Costa Rica successfully hosted the FIFA U-17 Women's World Cup 2014 and were celebrating further with their first ever qualification to the finals of the senior competition.

final that followed left Avedissian lamenting the physical differences between the powerful Americans and his own players: "All you can do really when Abby Wambach is playing like this is to pray, pray that they don't get the ball to her," he joked after the striker had netted three headers in the final.

Yet what they lack in height, this Costa Rica group make up for in unity after having played together for several years now, and after qualification their former coach was anything but downhearted about the future.

"There is really no ceiling for women's football in the country," he declared, and

not without cause. Las Ticas have played at four FIFA youth tournaments since 2008. They have yet to progress to the knockout stages of these elite competitions, but the experience of playing as a group has been invaluable in forming the core of the current senior side.

Now that they have qualified for both the FIFA Women's World Cup 2015 and the Pan American Games that follow in Canada in July, that unity and their nation's development will surely see them continue onwards and upwards.

LOOK OUT FOR

DIANA SAENZ
Born: 15 April 1989
Position: Defender

A solid, right-sided player who takes her defensive responsibilities seriously but is always happy to attack when the opportunity arises. The fact that she was named in the CONCACAF Women's Championship 2014 Best XI was testament to her dependable, dogged performances. Known for her optimistic, positive outlook and lively personality. Will be a senior at the University of South Florida in 2015 and has been almost ever-present for the Bulls in her first three years.

GLORIANA VILLALOBOS
Born: 20 August 1999
Position: Midfielder

The year 2014 was momentous for this skilful player: captain at the FIFA U-17 Women's World Cup on home soil in March, starred in the U-20 edition in the summer and made her senior competitive debut, aged just 14, in the Central American Football Union (UNCAF) pre-qualifying tournament. A bundle of energy but also a fantastic innovator in the creative midfield role, her huge potential has drawn high praise, including from Costa Rica men's coach Jorge Pinto.

KATHERINE ALVARADO
Born: 11 April 1991
Position: Midfielder

The team's co-captain, she moved away from her village and family in the Gautuzu Valley to the capital San Jose to play football aged 13. Says the sacrifice was worth it to achieve her dreams of playing for her country – which she has done at a string of international tournaments, most prominently the FIFA U-17 Women's World Cup 2008 in New Zealand and the U-20 edition in Germany. Has also realized her ambition to play abroad, spending time in the Finnish league.

Moncton Stadium, with its capacity of just over 20,000, will have an exciting atmosphere when Group F kicks off there on 9 June

CANADA
2015

FIFA
WOMEN'S WORLD CUP

TM©

GROUP F

The two European sides, England and France, should be the strongest of this group. But how they both cope with Mexico and Colombia's contrasting styles and rhythm of play could dictate their destiny in a competition in which France are tipped to go far.

FRANCE
CAN LES BLEUES PLAY TO PERFECTION IN CANADA?

France qualified for their third FIFA Women's World Cup with a flawless campaign, although their manager Philippe Bergeroo insisted they would keep their feet on the ground in the lead-up to 2015.

COACH

PHILIPPE BERGEROO

Made his name in men's football, playing in goal for Bordeaux and Toulouse. Won three caps for France and was a member of the 1984 gold medal-winning UEFA European Championship squad and on the roster for the 1986 FIFA World Cup in Mexico when Les Bleus finished third. Was goalkeeping coach for France's senior men's team, most notably with their 1998 FIFA World Cup-winning side, and went on to work domestically with Paris Saint-Germain and Stade Rennais. Led France's under-17 boys to UEFA Euro glory before taking over the women's side in July 2013. The 61-year-old is big on organization, quick passing, intelligent distribution and hard work.

When the tournament kicks off, however, an entire nation will want them to hit the football turf running in the hope that they can build on their fourth-place finish of 2011 in Germany.

France recorded the same position at the Olympics in London a year later and an athletic squad lit up the UEFA Women's Euro 2013 as well with their fast one- and two-touch technique. Les Bleues felt they were unlucky not to progress beyond the quarter-finals of that tournament, their exit coming after a penalty shoot-out loss to Denmark.

They needed to regroup afterwards, not just mentally but as a unit, given that their coach Bruno Bini was replaced soon after their return by former professional goalkeeper Bergeroo. The switch has proved a productive one and under Bergeroo, who has set the players to work on their strength in a bid to equip them for the competitive rigours that lie in wait, they have found fresh impetus.

In March 2014 the talented French stormed to a Cyprus Cup title triumph and six months later they completed their impeccable FIFA Women's World Cup qualification campaign, scoring 54 goals while conceding three during the course of 10 straight wins.

"I'm very happy," Bergeroo said once

Packed with quality this French team is a joy to watch but a menace to play against.

KEY PLAYER

LOUISA NECIB
Born: 23 January 1987

Playmaking midfielder with a sublime touch, she is a graduate of France's youth set-up, making her senior tournament debut in the UEFA Women's Euro 2005. Shortlisted for the Golden Ball in the FIFA Women's World Cup 2011, she was credited as vital to France's exciting give-and-go style in the UEFA Women's Euro 2013 in Sweden. Made the 10 best open-play goal list after she turned England's defence inside out and scored in the group stages; later named in the tournament's All-star squad. Has won the UEFA Women's Champions League with Olympique Lyonnais as well as countless domestic titles. The 28-year-old has been described by the French media as the "female Zinedine Zidane" and by her former manager Bruno Bini as "an artist".

WOMEN'S WORLD CUP RECORD

Year	Venue	Result
1991	China	Did not qualify
1995	Sweden	Did not qualify
1999	USA	Did not qualify
2003	USA	Group stage (3rd, Group B)
2007	China	Did not qualify
2011	Germany	Fourth place

qualification had been assured with a 2–0 victory away to Finland. "The first box is ticked. We now have a full year to work. We'll stay grounded because there is a long way to go."

France certainly worked hard throughout qualification, playing friendlies with heavyweights such as Sweden, Brazil and the USA. The Swedes were overcome 3–0, a goalless draw was played out against the South Americans, while France recorded a draw and a loss away to the USA. A strong Les Bleues team also tested themselves against Germany in October 2014, and Brazil, again, in November, emerging 2–0 victors in both games.

Results such as these will have been a fillip for Bergeroo, who is benefiting from the coming of age of a host of France's former youth players from the last decade, who play their domestic football in France's highly rated Division 1 Feminine.

Should France take their 2014 vein of form into 2015 and Canada, Les Bleues could make their coach and their nation even happier.

LOOK OUT FOR

GRIEDGE MBOCK BATHY
Born: 26 February 1995
Position: Defender

She was superb in the FIFA U-17 Women's World Cup in 2012 as Les Bleuettes won the trophy and she captured the Golden Ball. Hailed by FIFA's technical experts for her strength, reading of the game and aerial threat. Captained France to UEFA European Women's Under-19 Championship glory in 2013. She already has experience of playing in Canada – skippered France to third in the FIFA U-20 Women's World Cup in 2014.

WENDIE RENARD
Born: 20 July 1990
Position: Defender

Tall, elegant and strong defender who has developed into a fine captain for club and country. Reads the game well and can play in the centre or at full-back while offering a goal threat at set-pieces. Played in UEFA and FIFA tournaments with the under-19s and 20s and broke into the senior side in 2011, going on to play in that year's FIFA Women's World Cup and the 2012 Olympics. Has a wealth of experience in the UEFA Women's Champions League with Olympique Lyonnais.

EUGENIE LE SOMMER
Born: 18 May 1989
Position: Forward

Comes up with the goals in the big games but can also unlock defences and bring team-mates into play with her vision and precise passing. Named in the UEFA Women's Euro 2013 All-star squad and scored one of the top 10 best goals from open-play. Hit seven goals in eight Canada 2015 qualifiers. Crowned 2010 female player of the year by French National Union of Professional Football Players and won the Bronze Ball at the FIFA U-20 Women's World Cup in 2008.

ENGLAND
LIONESSES ROARING THEIR WAY TO CANADA

England surged towards qualification for the FIFA Women's World Cup with a 100 per cent record. They have reached the quarter-finals three times before – but can they beat that in 2015?

COACH

MARK SAMPSON

The 32-year-old Welshman was appointed in December 2013. Had been head coach at FA Women's Super League side Bristol Academy for five years, leading them to two FA Women's Cup finals and to a WSL runners-up berth in his final season. Started to learn his coaching trade in Wales and worked under Roberto Martinez at Swansea City AFC's Centre of Excellence. Martinez is just one of the coaches he cites as a major influence on his coaching style, which seeks to create an environment that encourages creativity. He says: "We want to be brave and have courage to control our own destiny."

The Three Lionesses will certainly head to North America with their tails up, having booked their ticket with such aplomb – scoring a whopping 52 goals and conceding only one along the way.

Belarus, Turkey, Montenegro, Ukraine and neighbours Wales were swept aside in qualification, with Olha Ovdiychuk's solitary goal for Ukraine the only blot on the otherwise perfect copybook of a campaign that went smoothly from first to last.

The Three Lionesses went into qualification on the back of a desperately disappointing display in Sweden at the UEFA Women's Euro 2013, where they suffered two defeats and a draw and went out in the group stage despite high expectations. The FA chose to end manager Hope Powell's era-defining 15-year reign and up stepped assistant Brent Hills as interim manager.

With zest and confidence returning to their performances, the players put six and eight goals past Belarus and Turkey respectively without reply. By the time The FA announced Powell's permanent replacement, former Bristol Academy WFC boss Mark Sampson, in December 2013, England were four wins in, top of the group and sitting pretty.

Even so, with the change of staff came a shift in approach and a shake-up in playing personnel too; a return to full fitness and

The Three Lionesses line-up has been refreshed under Mark Sampson and they are looking to compete with the best.

KEY PLAYER

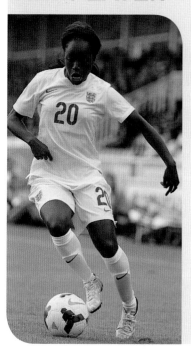

ENIOLA ALUKO
Born: 21 February 1987

A striker capable of frighteningly fast acceleration (like her professional-footballer younger brother, Sone) and very quick feet who can operate through the centre or more often down the right. Made her senior debut in 2004 and her first big impact for England in the UEFA Women's Euro 2005. She enjoyed a notable qualifying campaign, bagging 13 goals, concluding with her first international hat-trick in the 10–0 away demolition of Montenegro. Three seasons in the US Women's Professional Soccer league and then playing alongside other world greats at Chelsea has seen her mature into a dangerous weapon in Sampson's England armoury. A confident Aluko is more than a handful for even the best of defences.

WOMEN'S WORLD CUP RECORD

Year	Venue	Result
1991	China	Did not qualify
1995	Sweden	Quarter-finalists
1999	USA	Did not qualify
2003	USA	Did not qualify
2007	China	Quarter-finalists
2011	Germany	Quarter-finalists

form of several regulars was complemented by a willingness to try out younger and returning players.

Figures like striker Lianne Sanderson, who was starring for Boston Breakers in the US National Women's Soccer League, were brought back into the fold. Others, like midfielder Jordan Nobbs and defenders Lucy Bronze and Demi Stokes, were promoted into the side from the bench and the under-23s as regular starters.

Francesca Kirby, playing in the second tier of English football at Reading, was another to be given a chance and she rewarded Sampson's faith with a goal on her full debut in a friendly against Sweden in August 2014.

In qualifying, instinctive striker Toni Duggan notched up a 10-goal tally to prove her potential to lead the line for England into the future. Meanwhile Eniola Aluko's 13 strikes served as further evidence of a player at her peak.

Sampson regularly reiterates the importance of character, mentality and a positive attitude, and with buy-in from players, it can and has created a potent mix.

LOOK OUT FOR

STEPHANIE HOUGHTON
Born: 23 April 1988
Position: Defender

Steph Houghton became a household name after a great showing for Team GB at the London 2012 Olympic Games. England's new captain under Sampson, having been moved inside from left full-back to centre-back – a position she has also settled into playing for club side Manchester City WFC. A versatile all-rounder, her determination, leadership qualities and eye for goal make her an important part of the England side.

JORDAN NOBBS
Born: 8 December 1992
Position: Midfielder

A diminutive, dynamic, box-to-box midfielder, great striker of the ball with fantastic balance and poise. At just 15 she captained England at the FIFA U-17 Women's World Cup 2008 and scored in England's victory over Sweden in the final of the 2009 UEFA European Women's Under-19 Championship. Made her senior debut in March 2013 but really got her chance under Hills and played her part in qualification despite suffering a back injury in early 2014.

KAREN CARNEY
Born: 1 August 1987
Position: Forward

If Kelly Smith is the most gifted female player to hail from England, then Carney must be the closest to follow in her creative footsteps. Debuted for England a decade ago and plays with passion, whether dribbling down the left flank or pulling the strings in midfield. Enjoyed spells in the US at Chicago Red Stars and in England with Arsenal, where she won plenty of silverware. Returned to first club Birmingham City where she won the FA Women's Cup in 2012.

COLOMBIA
COLLECTIVE AMBITION GIVES COLOMBIA CAUSE FOR OPTIMISM

Colombia booked their second FIFA Women's World Cup berth by being one of the top two sides in the Copa America Femenina tournament. Their coach says they are as close as a family – so how far can their cohesion carry them in Canada?

COACH

FABIAN FELIPE TABORDA

"El Profesor" became a part of Colombia's women's set-up in 2012 when he took responsibility for Las Cafeteritas, as the youth sides are known. Took the under-20s to a gold medal finish in the regional multi-sport Bolivarian Games in 2013 and led the younger girls to the 2012 and 2014 FIFA U-17 Women's World Cups. Got the senior job in 2014 and oversaw an unbeaten campaign in qualification for Canada 2015 via the Copa America Femenina. The 36-year-old also has experience at league level in Colombia as technical director of the women's section of Club Deportivo Generaciones Palmiranas, where several of his national squad play their football.

It took them to great heights in the Copa America Femenina in September 2014 when they finished as the only unbeaten team after facing Uruguay, Venezuela, Peru, Argentina, Brazil and hosts Ecuador.

Las Cafeteras boasted the meanest defence in that competition too, conceding twice in seven games and denying Brazil the chance to score in the final match, a goalless draw that booked both nations a spot in Canada 2015.

Their second-place finish in the final-phase group table additionally saw Colombia through to the 2015 Pan American Games, also in Canada, and the 2016 Olympics in Brazil. For now, though, the South American side are looking towards the biggest women's tournament in the FIFA calendar and their second stab at world glory.

Colombia took a point from a tough group in the 2011 edition, drawing with Korea DPR but losing to highly rated Sweden and eventual finalists the USA. Not particularly physical on the field, the squad relied instead on skill, organization and discipline to get them through and although they did not get out of their group they left Germany that year with their heads held high.

Colombia were disappointed to lose every match in the London 2012 Olympics

Colombia's team are like a family of sisters, all of whom are great with a ball at their feet.

KEY PLAYER

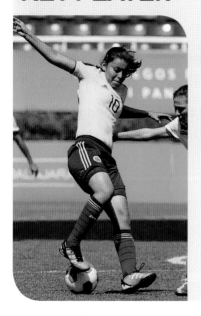

YORELI RINCON
Born: 27 July 1993

The No. 10 has been labelled Colombia's answer to Marta and the comparison is not without justification. A vibrant and exciting player, she is totally at ease with the ball at her feet. Taught to play by her brother, she has gone on to gain experience of FIFA U-17 and U-20 Women's World Cups with her country. Made the All-star team in the 2010 U-20 edition for her skills as a playmaker. Will still only be 21 when Canada 2015 kicks off – but already has a wealth of experience, having played at club level in Brazil, Sweden and America. Scored key goals to secure Colombia's place in both the 2011 and 2015 FIFA Women's World Cups and will be a crowd-pleaser in Canada.

WOMEN'S WORLD CUP RECORD

Year	Venue	Result
1991	China	Did not enter
1995	Sweden	Did not enter
1999	USA	Did not qualify
2003	USA	Did not qualify
2007	China	Did not qualify
2011	Germany	Group stage (4th, Group C)

– but their opponents did include stellar footballing nations France and the USA.

Las Cafeteras had some rising stars of their own in those two competitions, including several from the tight-knit group who had experienced the FIFA U-20 Women's World Cup 2010 together.

Gifted strikers Lady Andrade and Ingrid Vidal, reliable defender and inspirational skipper Natalia Gaitan and attacking midfielder Tatiana Ariza are just a few to have graduated from the youth teams to become regulars for the national side.

Several new faces were bedded in during qualification too – all of which bodes well for the future of this increasingly impressive footballing nation.

"We have a close-knit team as in a family," said coach Fabian Felipe Taborda, who took over from Ricardo Rozo in 2014. "We are a team that plays good football and we are mentally tough."

That strong mindset has seen Las Cafeteras through to Canada 2015; Colombians will hope that they can maintain that outlook to perform at an even higher level when their tournament begins.

LOOK OUT FOR

NATALIA GAITAN
Born: 3 April 1991
Position: Defender

She may be small in stature but this player rises to every occasion with her bravery and technical ability. Skippered her country at youth level before assuming the captaincy of the seniors, leading them in the FIFA Women's World Cup 2011 when aged just 20. Played every minute of their three matches in Germany and was noted for having led her side in a rousing sing-song in the tunnel before their opening match against Sweden. Also captained the side in the London 2012 Olympics and commands the respect of her peers.

NATALY ARIAS
Born: 2 April 1986
Position: Defender

Was an All-American midfielder at school, where she bagged tons of goals and almost as many plaudits. Captained the Terrapins women's soccer team at the University of Maryland and joined up with Colombia's national side in 2010. Played in the FIFA Women's World Cup 2011 and the Pan American Games later that year, as well as the London 2012 Olympic Games. She featured at right-back, and continues to impress in that position, where she is solid defensively and loves to get forward.

LADY ANDRADE
Born: 10 January 1992
Position: Midfielder/Forward

Lively player who loves nothing more than a chance to show off her dribbling skills and tricks on the big stage. Was a hit at the FIFA U-20 Women's World Cup in 2010 and made the All-star team after impressing with her ability to take players on. Still a youngster but has experience of senior international and high-level club football, having played in the FIFA Women's World Cup 2011 and London 2012 Olympics, and in both the Copa Libertadores Femenina and the UEFA Women's Champions League.

MEXICO

LAS TRICOLORES LOOK TO BUILD ON EXPERIENCE IN CANADA

Mexico have grown in stature in the world game since the first national women's league was set up in the late 1990s. This rising football nation will look to kick on again in this, their third FIFA Women's World Cup.

COACH

LEONARDO CUELLAR

A former international midfielder who represented Mexico at the 1978 FIFA World Cup in Argentina. Played for several teams in the North American Soccer League during his career and was coaching the men's team at California State University, Los Angeles, when he was tasked with developing the women's game and coaching the national team in Mexico in the late 1990s. His dedication and enthusiasm has not wavered since. His son Christopher coaches the under-20s and Leo is his assistant. Obsessive about the game, he once declared: "Football is my life!"

Previous outings in the tournament have shown Mexico's ability to progress as they have gone from failing to take a single point in 1999 to recording two from a brace of draws in 2011.

Coach Leonardo Cuellar, in charge of the national side in both the 1999 and 2011 editions, steered Las Tricolores to the world stage once more in 2015 and he is eager for Mexico to attain even better results this time.

"Our qualification has brought a sense of joy and relief," he said. "I am very proud of the team and the federation's commitment to women's soccer. We want to keep learning."

So far, Mexico have proved worthy scholars, the country transforming from one that once found it difficult to raise a

national women's side to one that now boasts teams capable of holding their own at all levels.

Las Tri reached the FIFA U-20 Women's World Cup quarter-finals in 2010 and 2012, and that feat was equalled by the under-17s in their edition of the competition in 2014.

The senior side is now packed with graduates from those U-20 tournaments and they were utilized to good effect in their regional qualifying competition, the CONCACAF Women's Championship, in October 2014.

Although Mexico stuttered in their opener

Mexico are as dedicated to developing their game as their long-serving coach Leonardo Cuellar.

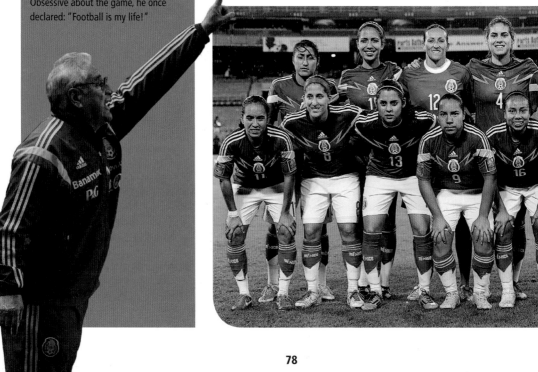

KEY PLAYER

ALINA GARCIAMENDEZ
Born: 16 April 1991

Texas-raised central defender who is strong in the air, technically impressive and a natural leader. She was a stand-out success for Stanford University during her college career. A star for Mexico's under-20s side, she scored against Nigeria in the FIFA U-20 Women's World Cup 2010 to level the match 1–1 and see her team through to the knockout stages, for the first time, as group winners. A starter for Mexico in the FIFA Women's World Cup 2011, she has played in the German Frauen-Bundesliga with 1. FFC Frankfurt, where her team-mates included FIFA Women's World Cup 2007 winners Fatmire Alushi and Melanie Behringer. Is studying at a dental school in Texas.

WOMEN'S WORLD CUP RECORD

Year	Venue	Result
1991	China	Did not qualify
1995	Sweden	Did not qualify
1999	USA	Group stage (4th, Group B)
2003	USA	Did not qualify
2007	China	Did not qualify
2011	Germany	Group stage (3rd, Group B)

with a 1–0 loss to Costa Rica, Cuellar shuffled his pack and they went on to demolish Martinique 10–0 before disposing of Jamaica 3–1. The coach rested players in the semi-final against the USA, which ended in a 3–0 defeat, but that decision ultimately paid dividends when his team beat Trinidad and Tobago in extra time in the match for third place.

That result assured Mexico of a berth in Canada 2015 and Cuellar said he hoped his squad would do their confederation proud on the world stage.

Mexico still have some way to go to make the kind of impact that fellow CONCACAF representatives the USA have had on the competition. Yet with many of his players competing for American colleges or in

that country's National Women's Soccer League, Las Tricolores are learning fast. And although the squad are less physically imposing than their rivals, they counter any potential shortfall with tenacity and technique.

When they run out in Canada this summer, Cuellar's ever-improving squad just might teach the world a few lessons of their own.

LOOK OUT FOR

VERONICA PEREZ
Born: 18 May 1988
Position: Midfielder

Hails from California and appeared for the USA under-23s. Switched to Mexico in 2009 and ironically scored the winning goal for Las Tri in their 2–1 semi-final win over the Stars and Stripes in the CONCACAF Women's World Cup qualifying competition in 2010. Helps build attacks but also likes to get forward with dangerous runs into the penalty area. Has played college soccer for the University of Washington's Huskies and professionally in America with three different teams.

MARIBEL DOMINGUEZ
Born: 18 November 1978
Position: Forward

Pretended to be a boy so that she could play the beautiful game as a child in Mexico City. Played in the FIFA Women's World Cup 1999 in the USA and has now accrued well over 100 caps. Sometimes referred to as "Marigol" for her scoring exploits, she holds the distinction of being the only player to have scored for Mexico in the Olympic Games, FIFA Women's World Cup, CONCACAF Women's Championship and Pan American Games. She is credited with making football popular in her homeland.

MONICA OCAMPO
Born: 4 January 1987
Position: Forward

A clever footballer with a sweet left foot – although it was with her right that she scored a stunning long-range equalizer against England in the FIFA Women's World Cup 2011. She is reliable in front of goal and will take her chances when they come. Has forged a career across the border, firstly in the USA's W-League before turning out for Women's Professional Soccer league side Atlanta Beat and Sky Blue FC in the National Women's Soccer League. Was top scorer for Sky Blue in 2013.

FIFA WOMEN'S WORLD CUP HISTORY

The first official FIFA Women's World Cup was held in China in 1991, with just 12 teams present. Although Canada will host only the seventh edition of the tournament, many memorable moments and stars have been created in its 24-year history. In total, 24 national teams have featured in the finals, playing in 180 matches. This section chronicles every result and group table — from the USA's triumphant "triple-edged sword" attack in 1991 to Japan's penalty shoot-out heroines in 2011.

One of the most iconic images of FIFA Women's World Cups past – a shirtless Brandi Chastain drops to her knees in celebration of her trophy winning penalty kick in 1999.

FIFA WOMEN'S WORLD CUP CHINA 1991

Following the success of the FIFA 1988 International Women's Tournament in China, teams returned to Guangdong three years later to compete for the first official world title.

Women's football captured the public imagination on a global scale in 1991 when the inaugural official FIFA Women's World Championship kicked off in China. More than half a million fans turned out to watch 12 teams compete for honours across five stadiums in Guangdong province in the south-east of China.

The final, between pre-tournament favourites USA and Norway at Guangzhou's Tianhe Stadium, remains one of the most nail-biting in the 24-year history of the competition. Matches were 80 minutes long for this tournament rather than football's standard 90 and the battle between the Stars and Stripes and their greatest rivals was so close that extra time was almost needed.

Star player and tournament Golden Shoe winner Michelle Akers had got Anson Dorrance's USA off to a flying start 20 minutes into the final with a stupendous header but Norway's leading scorer of the tournament, Linda Medalen, equalized nine minutes later. The 63,000 spectators watched breathlessly as the game remained deadlocked and the clock ticked down, but with two minutes to go Akers leapt on a weak Norwegian back-pass to side-foot into

Julie Foudy (left), Michelle Akers (centre) and player of the tournament, Carin Jennings lift the trophy and a bouquet of flowers.

an empty net and secure a historic victory for the USA.

Italy striker Carolina Morace, who would go on to manage Canada at a FIFA Women's World Cup and coached a men's team in Italy's Serie C, made history when she hit the competition's first-ever hat-trick.

It was a historic tournament for women officials too, as female referees and assistants featured for the first time in a FIFA competition, with Claudia Vasconcelos of Brazil taking the whistle in the third-place play-off between Sweden and Germany.

That match finished 4–0 to the Scandinavians, whose roster included star striker Pia Sundhage, who 20 years later coached the USA in the FIFA Women's World Cup 2011. Germany, whose squad included a 27-year-old Silvia Neid, went on to lift the FIFA Fair Play award.

All told, 99 goals flew in during the 26 matches of the tournament, with the USA, featuring a 19-year-old Mia Hamm and 20-year-old students Julie Foudy and Kristine Lilly, top-scoring in the tournament with 25 while conceding just five.

Acrobatic action from Italy's 5–0 opening Group C rout of Chinese Taipei.

GROUP A

China PR	4	Norway	0
Denmark	3	New Zealand	0
China PR	2	Denmark	2
Norway	4	New Zealand	0
China PR	4	New Zealand	1
Norway	2	Denmark	1

	P	W	D	L	F	A	Pts
China PR	3	2	1	0	10	3	5
Norway	3	2	1	0	6	5	5
Denmark	3	1	1	1	6	4	3
New Zealand	3	0	0	3	1	11	0

GROUP B

Japan	0	Brazil	1
Sweden	2	USA	3
Japan	0	Sweden	8
Brazil	0	USA	5
Japan	0	USA	3
Brazil	0	Sweden	2

	P	W	D	L	F	A	Pts
USA	3	3	0	0	11	2	6
Sweden	3	2	0	1	12	3	4
Brazil	3	1	0	2	1	7	2
Japan	3	0	0	3	0	12	0

GROUP C

Chinese Taipei	0	Italy	5
Germany	4	Nigeria	0
Chinese Taipei	0	Germany	3
Italy	1	Nigeria	0
Chinese Taipei	2	Nigeria	0
Italy	0	Germany	2

	P	W	D	L	F	A	Pts
Germany	3	3	0	0	9	0	6
Italy	3	2	0	1	6	2	4
Chinese Taipei	3	1	0	2	2	8	2
Nigeria	3	0	0	3	0	7	0

QUARTER-FINALS

China PR	0	Sweden	1
Norway	3	Italy	2*
Denmark	1	Germany	2*
USA	7	Chinese Taipei	0

* After extra time

SEMI-FINALS

Sweden	1	Norway	4
Germany	2	USA	5

THIRD-PLACE MATCH

Sweden	4	Germany	0

FINAL – 30 November: Tianhe Stadium, Guangzhou

Norway	1	USA	2
Medalen (29)		Akers (20)	
		Akers (78)	

H-T: 1–1   Att: 63,000   Ref: Zhuk (Belarus)

Norway: Seth, Zaborowski (Straedet 79), Espeseth, Nyborg, Carlsen, Haugen, Store, Riise, Medalen, Hegstad, Svensson
USA: Harvey, Heinrichs, Higgins, Overbeck, Hamilton, Hamm, Akers, Foudy, Jennings, Lilly, Fawcett
Top scorers: 10 Akers (USA), 7 Mohr (Germany), 6 Medalen (Norway), 6 Jennings (USA)

FIFA WOMEN'S WORLD CUP SWEDEN 1995

A long-time hotbed of women's football, Sweden proved enthusiastic hosts when the second global tournament came to Europe and Scandinavia provided the first European winners.

"The future is feminine," declared then FIFA General Secretary Joseph S. Blatter after the second edition of the FIFA Women's World Cup had come to a close in Sweden in the summer of 1995.

His suggestion was not without foundation: more than 110,000 supporters had just witnessed 26 keenly contested matches between 12 of the world's top women's sides. Up-and-coming stars such as China PR's Sun Wen, USA's Mia Hamm and Germany's Maren Meinert had all graced the world stage with their skills.

Furthermore, Swedish official Ingrid Jonsson had become the first woman to referee a FIFA final, while two of the game's future greats, then-teenagers Birgit Prinz of Germany and Japan's Homare Sawa, tasted a World Cup environment for the very first time.

Parity with the men's game had come, too, with matches now lasting 90 minutes – and supporters across Sweden savoured every moment of them as 99 goals billowed into the nets in the space of two weeks.

The hosts did not feature for the full fortnight of competition, however. Despite bouncing back from a shock opening-match defeat by Brazil, Sweden were eliminated by China in the quarter-finals in the first-ever FIFA Women's World Cup match to be decided by penalties.

England, whose squad featured future

Germany striker Heidi Mohr and Brazil's Cenira compete for the ball, as Sissi looks on in Germany's 6-1 Group stage win.

manager Hope Powell, and Japan were beaten by Germany and the USA in their quarters, which left Denmark needing to overcome Norway.

It was quite an ask: the Norwegians had powered their way through the group stage, hitting 17 goals without reply and though Denmark scored the only goal Norway would concede, they lost the quarter-final 3–1.

Spurred on by vociferous Scandinavian support, Norway went on to avenge their 1991 final defeat to USA in the semis, Golden Shoe winner Ann Kristin Aarones scoring the only goal to beat the holders.

China PR's hopes of reaching this edition's final, meanwhile, were dashed in the 88th minute of their semi against Germany when Bettina Wiegmann popped up to score the winner.

The rain fell steadily on the first all-European FIFA Women's World Cup final but nothing could dampen Norway's title tilt which was settled by goals from the supremely gifted midfielder Hege Riise and a 20-year-old Marianne Pettersen in front of more than 17,000 fans.

Norway's "supremely gifted" midfielder Hege Riise gets her hands on the coveted prize.

GROUP A

Sweden	0		Brazil				1
Germany	1		Japan				0
Sweden	3		Germany				2
Brazil	1		Japan				2
Sweden	2		Japan				0
Brazil	1		Germany				6

	P	W	D	L	F	A	Pts
Germany	3	2	0	1	9	4	6
Sweden	3	2	0	1	5	3	6
Japan	3	1	0	2	2	4	3
Brazil	3	1	0	2	3	8	3

GROUP B

Norway	8	Nigeria	0
England	3	Canada	2
Norway	2	England	0
Nigeria	3	Canada	3
Norway	7	Canada	0
Nigeria	2	England	3

	P	W	D	L	F	A	Pts
Norway	3	3	0	0	17	0	9
England	3	2	0	1	6	6	6
Canada	3	0	1	2	5	13	1
Nigeria	3	0	1	2	5	14	1

GROUP C

USA	3	China PR	3
Denmark	5	Australia	0
USA	2	Denmark	0
China PR	4	Australia	2
USA	4	Australia	1
China PR	3	Denmark	1

	P	W	D	L	F	A	Pts
USA	3	2	1	0	9	4	7
China PR	3	2	1	0	10	6	7
Denmark	3	1	0	2	6	5	3
Australia	3	0	0	3	3	13	0

QUARTER-FINALS

Germany	3	England	0
Sweden	1 (3)	China PR	1 (4)*
Japan	0	USA	4
Norway	3	Denmark	1

* After extra time (pens)

SEMI-FINALS

Germany	1	China PR	0
USA	0	Norway	1

THIRD-PLACE MATCH

China PR	0	USA	2

FINAL – 18 June: Rasunda Stadium, Solna

Germany	0	Norway	2
		Riise (37)	
		Pettersen (40)	
H-T: 0–2	Att: 17,158	Ref: Jonsson (Sweden)	

Germany: Goller, Bernhard, Austermuhl, Pohlmann (Wunderlich 75), Lohn, Meinert (Smisek 86), Voss-Tecklenburg, Wiegmann, Mohr, Neid, Prinz (Brocker 42)
Norway: Nordby, Svensson, Espeseth, A. Nymark Andersen, N. Nymark Andersen, Riise, Haugen, Medalen, Aarones, Myklebust, Pettersen
Top scorers: 6 Aarones (Norway), 5 Riise (Norway)

FIFA WOMEN'S WORLD CUP USA 1999

With two years of planning and marketing behind the promotion of the FIFA Women's World Cup, the USA's organisers believed that the 1999 competition could be big. Boy, were they right.

As breakthrough competitions go, the third edition of the FIFA Women's World Cup has to rank among the most significant.

The USA went all-out to make this tournament a success and the public responded with the same enthusiasm: spectators filed through the turnstiles in their hundreds of thousands, host cities embraced visiting teams and television viewers tuned in to watch the tournament in their millions. Women's football was on the map and deservedly so.

Hosts and reigning Olympic champions the USA scored 18 goals and conceded just three on their road to a gripping final against China PR. Brazil's flair player Sissi and China's shining talent Sun Wen bagged seven goals apiece to jointly claim the Golden Shoe.

In total, a whacking 123 goals were scored across the board as the 16 teams played their hearts out under the most intense public gaze and media glare yet experienced in the women's game.

Oh, and USA midfielder Brandi Chastain whipped off her shirt after scoring the winning penalty in the final against China to create an iconic and enduring image in 20th-century sport.

The USA did not have it all their own way on home turf, though. The Stars and Stripes had to come back from 2–1 down to beat reigning European champions Germany in

This is what 90,185 fans at a FIFA Women's World Cup Final looks like.

the quarter-finals.

Tony DiCicco's team were back in their stride in the semi-finals, easing past Brazil, who had enjoyed the tournament of their lives after winning just once in each of the previous two FIFA Women's World Cups.

China saw off Russia 2–0 in the quarters and they blitzed holders Norway 5–0 in the semi on 4 July in Foxborough en route to the final. That defeat brought an end to the Norwegians' remarkable record of 10 straight FIFA Women's World Cup victories.

Finalists China and the USA eventually each met their match when they went head to head in the 1994 FIFA World Cup final venue, the Rose Bowl in Pasadena, six days later.

China had lost 2–1 to the USA in the first-ever Women's Olympic final three years earlier on American soil. But in the 1999 final there was little to choose between the two as 90,185 spectators (a record for a women's sporting event) were kept on the edge of their seats into extra time and penalties, with the match and the title settled in the USA's favour thanks to a Briana Scurry save and Chastain's coolness under pressure.

FIFA President Sepp Blatter and President/CEO of the FIFA Women's World Cup 1999 Organizing Committee Marla Messing are crowded out by the raised arms of the victorious US team.

GROUP A

USA	3	Denmark	0
Korea DPR	1	Nigeria	2
USA	7	Nigeria	1
Korea DPR	3	Denmark	1
USA	3	Korea DPR	0
Nigeria	2	Denmark	0

	P	W	D	L	F	A	Pts
USA	3	3	0	0	13	1	9
Nigeria	3	2	0	1	5	8	6
Korea DPR	3	1	0	2	4	6	3
Denmark	3	0	0	3	1	8	0

GROUP B

Germany	1	Italy	1
Brazil	7	Mexico	1
Germany	6	Mexico	0
Brazil	2	Italy	0
Germany	3	Brazil	3
Mexico	0	Italy	1

	P	W	D	L	F	A	Pts
Brazil	3	2	1	0	12	4	7
Germany	3	1	2	0	10	4	5
Italy	3	1	1	1	3	3	4
Mexico	3	0	0	3	1	15	0

GROUP C

Norway	2	Russia	1
Japan	1	Canada	1
Norway	7	Canada	1
Japan	0	Russia	5
Norway	4	Japan	0
Canada	1	Russia	4

	P	W	D	L	F	A	Pts
Norway	3	3	0	0	13	2	9
Russia	3	2	0	1	10	3	6
Canada	3	0	1	2	3	12	1
Japan	3	0	1	2	1	10	1

GROUP D

China PR	2	Sweden	1
Australia	1	Ghana	1
China PR	7	Ghana	0
Australia	1	Sweden	3
China PR	3	Australia	1
Ghana	0	Sweden	2

	P	W	D	L	F	A	Pts
China PR	3	3	0	0	12	2	9
Sweden	3	2	0	1	6	3	6
Australia	3	0	1	2	3	7	1
Ghana	3	0	1	2	1	10	1

QUARTER-FINALS

USA	3	Germany	2
Brazil	4	Nigeria	3*
Norway	3	Sweden	1
China PR	2	Russia	0

* After extra time

SEMI-FINALS

USA	2	Brazil	0
Norway	0	China PR	5

THIRD-PLACE MATCH

Brazil	0 (5)	Norway	0 (4)*

* On penalties

FINAL – 10 July: Rose Bowl, Pasadena

USA	0 (5)	China PR	0 (4)	After extra time (on penalties)
H-T: 0–0; F-T: 0–0		Att: 90,185		Ref: Petignat (Switzerland)

USA: Scurry, Overbeck, Chastain, Hamm, Akers (Whalen 91), Foudy, Parlow (MacMillan 57), Lilly, Fawcett, Milbrett (Venturini 115), Markgraf
China PR: Gao, Wang, Fan, Zhao (Qiu 114), Jin (Xie 119), Sun, Liu A., Pu (Zhang 59), Wen, Liu Y., Bai
Top scorers: 7 Sun (China PR), 7 Sissi (Brazil), 4 Aarones (Norway)

FIFA WOMEN'S WORLD CUP USA 2003

The USA stepped in at a late stage to host the best teams from around the world for a second successive occasion but it would not be a case of repeated success for them on the field.

The 2003 SARS virus crisis that affected chosen hosts China meant that in the May of that year the FIFA Women's World Cup finals were reluctantly switched to the USA.

It was the second consecutive time that America had played host – and that autumn the USA rose to the challenge. Despite the tournament clashing with the wildly popular American football and baseball seasons, the crowds still came in their hundreds of thousands to watch the women in venues in the east and west of the country.

They were richly rewarded – thirty-somethings Sun Wen of China PR, Germany's Maren Meinert and Mia Hamm of the USA continued to thrill, but legends in the making such as Brazil's Marta, the USA's Abby Wambach and Germany's Kerstin Garefrekes also stood out despite their relative youth.

There were new faces among the 16 teams too, with France, Korea Republic and Argentina making their FIFA Women's World Cup debuts.

The usual suspects – USA, Germany, Norway, Sweden and China – all progressed to the quarter-finals. Russia, whose squad included the youngest player of the tournament in 16-year-old talent Elena Danilova, also made the last eight, along with Brazil and Canada, the North Americans progressing beyond the group

Golden goal-scorer Nia Kunzer puts her hands to her head in disbelief as she reacts to winning the 2003 final.

stages for the first time.

The Canucks, with 20-year-old star striker Christine Sinclair leading the line, ended China's World Cup with a 1–0 quarter-final victory in only their second win over the Steel Roses, who went on to collect the FIFA Fair Play award.

Germany signalled their intent with a 7–1 demolition of Russia in Portland and the USA saw off old adversaries Norway with lively new prospect Wambach scoring the only goal. Sweden beat Brazil 2–1 although a 17-year-old Marta kept a cool head, despite her tender years, to score from the spot.

In the semi-finals in Portland, Germany eliminated USA 3–0, inflicting only the second-ever FIFA Women's World Cup defeat on the hosts. Canada's dreams of a final on US soil were ended by Sweden who came back from behind with two late goals.

The winning goal for Germany in the final against Sweden in Los Angeles was of the golden variety, Nia Kunzer scoring a powerful header in the 98th minute to cap off a German fightback.

It was only the second golden goal ever to be scored at a FIFA Women's World Cup and it would be the last, but what a crucial goal it was.

Established stars such as Mia Hamm combined with emerging talents like her USA strike partner Abby Wambach.

GROUP A

Nigeria	0	Korea DPR	3
USA	3	Sweden	1
Sweden	1	Korea DPR	0
USA	5	Nigeria	0
Sweden	3	Nigeria	0
Korea DPR	0	USA	3

	P	W	D	L	F	A	Pts
USA	3	3	0	0	11	1	9
Sweden	3	2	0	1	5	3	6
Korea DPR	3	1	0	2	3	4	3
Nigeria	3	0	0	3	0	11	0

GROUP B

Norway	2	France	0
Brazil	3	Korea Republic	0
Norway	1	Brazil	4
France	1	Korea Republic	0
Korea Republic	1	Norway	7
France	1	Brazil	1

	P	W	D	L	F	A	Pts
Brazil	3	2	1	0	8	2	7
Norway	3	2	0	1	10	5	6
France	3	1	1	1	2	3	4
Korea Republic	3	0	0	3	1	11	0

GROUP C

Germany	4	Canada	1
Japan	6	Argentina	0
Germany	3	Japan	0
Canada	3	Argentina	0
Canada	3	Japan	1
Argentina	1	Germany	6

	P	W	D	L	F	A	Pts
Germany	3	3	0	0	13	2	9
Canada	3	2	0	1	7	5	6
Japan	3	1	0	2	7	6	3
Argentina	3	0	0	3	1	15	0

GROUP D

Australia	1	Russia	2
China PR	1	Ghana	0
Ghana	0	Russia	3
China PR	1	Australia	1
Ghana	2	Australia	1
China PR	1	Russia	0

	P	W	D	L	F	A	Pts
China PR	3	2	1	0	3	1	7
Russia	3	2	0	1	5	2	6
Ghana	3	1	0	2	2	5	3
Australia	3	0	1	2	3	5	1

QUARTER-FINALS

USA	1	Norway	0
Brazil	1	Sweden	2
Germany	7	Russia	1
China PR	0	Canada	1

SEMI-FINALS

| USA | 0 | Germany | 3 |
| Sweden | 2 | Canada | 1 |

THIRD-PLACE MATCH

| USA | 3 | Canada | 1 |

FINAL – 12 October: Home Depot Center, Carson

Germany	2	Sweden	1	After extra time
Meinert (46)		Ljungberg (41)		
Kunzer (98)				

H-T: 0–1; **F-T:** 1–1   **Att:** 26,137   **Ref:** Babadac (Romania)

Germany: Rottenberg, Stegemann, Lingor, Wunderlich (Kunzer 88), Prinz, Wiegmann, Minnert, Meinert, Hingst, Garefrekes (Muller 76), Gottschlich
Sweden: Jonsson, Westberg, Tornqvist, Marklund, Mostrom, Larsson (Bengtsson 76), Andersson (Sjogran 53), Ljungberg, Svensson, Sjostrom (Fagerstrom 53), Ostberg
Top scorers: 7 Prinz (Germany), 4 Meinert (Germany), 4 Katia (Brazil), 4 Garefrekes (Germany)

FIFA WOMEN'S WORLD CUP CHINA 2007

The fifth edition was played in Asia, and around a million spectators witnessed the ever-improving standard and excitement of the women's game.

China PR finally got to stage the FIFA Women's World Cup again in the autumn of 2007 and the opening ceremony showed just how eagerly anticipated its arrival was.

Around a million spectators made their way through the turnstiles in venues across the country over the space of three weeks, and nearly 30,000 of them were lucky enough to get a ticket for the opening ceremony at Hongkou Stadium in Shanghai on 10 September. Before them

danced children inside giant footballs and cartoon socks and trainers, while above their heads leapt thunderous fireworks and multicoloured flashing lights.

The match that followed was a spectacle too, holders Germany keeping up the lustre by obliterating Argentina 11–0 with hat tricks from Birgit Prinz, in her fourth FIFA Women's World Cup, and Sandra Smisek.

Germany faced tougher competition in their second group match when they came

up against England, who were making their first appearance at a FIFA Women's World Cup finals in 12 years.

Three days previously, England's talismanic striker Kelly Smith had tugged off her boots and kissed them after scoring two beautiful goals in a 2–2 draw with Japan. But the

A snapshot of the hugely entertaining, quirky, yet lavish opening ceremony in Shanghai.

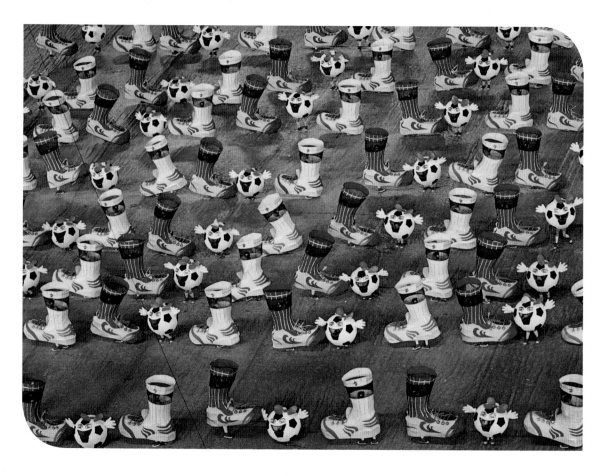

encounter with Germany remained goalless despite both sides' best efforts.

Germany enjoyed more success against Japan, winning 2–0 before breezing into the final with quarter and semi-final wins over Korea DPR and Norway respectively.

Norway had been the architects of China's downfall as the Steel Roses fell at the quarter-final stage, while Australia gave Brazil a scare in their quarter-final until Cristiane bagged the winner in the 75th minute.

The USA had made light work of their group and they did the same with England in the quarters, but they were beaten soundly by Brazil in the semis in a thrilling game of skills and spills that saw the Chinese fans roar on playmaker Marta in their thousands.

Golden Shoe and Golden Ball award winner Marta was unable to penetrate the powerhouse that was Germany in the final in Shanghai, even having a penalty saved by Nadine Angerer.

Prinz and Simone Laudehr bagged second-half goals to ensure that Germany, under Silvia Neid, became the first team to successfully defend the FIFA Women's World Cup title – and they did it without even conceding a goal.

Germany keeper Nadine Angerer keeps her remarkable shut-out record intact with a penalty save from Brazil's Marta in the final.

GROUP A

Germany	11	Argentina	0
Japan	2	England	2
Argentina	0	Japan	1
England	0	Germany	0
Germany	2	Japan	0
England	6	Argentina	1

	P	W	D	L	F	A	Pts
Germany	3	2	1	0	13	0	7
England	3	1	2	0	8	3	5
Japan	3	1	1	1	3	4	4
Argentina	3	0	0	3	1	18	0

GROUP B

USA	2	Korea DPR	2
Nigeria	1	Sweden	1
Sweden	0	USA	2
Korea DPR	2	Nigeria	0
Nigeria	0	USA	1
Korea DPR	1	Sweden	1

	P	W	D	L	F	A	Pts
USA	3	2	1	0	5	2	7
Korea DPR	3	1	1	1	5	4	4
Sweden	3	1	1	1	3	4	4
Nigeria	3	0	1	2	1	4	1

GROUP C

Ghana	1	Australia	4
Norway	2	Canada	1
Canada	4	Ghana	0
Australia	1	Norway	1
Norway	7	Ghana	2
Australia	2	Canada	1

	P	W	D	L	F	A	Pts
Norway	3	2	1	0	10	4	7
Australia	3	1	2	0	7	4	5
Canada	3	1	1	1	6	4	4
Ghana	3	0	0	3	3	15	0

GROUP D

New Zealand	0	Brazil	5
China PR	3	Denmark	2
Denmark	2	New Zealand	0
Brazil	4	China PR	0
China PR	2	New Zealand	0
Brazil	1	Denmark	0

	P	W	D	L	F	A	Pts
Brazil	3	3	0	0	10	0	9
China PR	3	2	0	1	5	6	6
Denmark	3	1	0	2	4	4	3
New Zealand	3	0	0	3	0	9	0

QUARTER-FINALS

Germany	3	Korea DPR	0
USA	3	England	0
Norway	1	China PR	0
Brazil	3	Australia	2

SEMI-FINALS

Germany	3	Norway	0
USA	0	Brazil	4

THIRD-PLACE MATCH

Norway	1	USA	4

FINAL – 30 September: Hongkou Football Stadium, Shanghai

Germany	2	Brazil	0

Prinz (52)
Laudehr (86)

H-T: 0–0   **Att:** 31,000   **Ref:** Ogston (Australia)

Germany: Angerer, Stegemann, Krahn, Bresonik, Behringer (Muller 74), Smisek (Alushi 80), Prinz, Lingor, Laudehr, Hingst, Garefrekes
Brazil: Andreia, Elaine, Aline (Katia 88), Tania (Pretinha 81), Renata Costa, Daniela, Formiga, Maycon, Marta, Cristiane, Ester (Rosana 63)
Top scorers: 7 Marta (Brazil), 6 Wambach (USA), 6 R. Gulbrandsen (Norway)

FIFA WOMEN'S WORLD CUP GERMANY 2011

With stands packed with noisy and colourful supporters, quality football throughout and a truly astonishing finale, Germany 2011 was an outstanding experience.

Title holders and firm favourites, Germany invited the world to enjoy another "summer fairytale" – promising to reprise the celebration of football that was the 2006 FIFA World Cup.

However, their dream of victory on home soil was not to be. Instead, another story-book ending was written and a new team joined the list of giants in the game, becoming only the fourth nation to be crowned world champions.

Inspired largely by the performances and goals of their captain Homare Sawa, Japan clinched victory on penalties after a sensational final in Frankfurt against USA.

The Nadeshiko were popular and fitting winners not simply because of their artful passing and pressing game – they had also given their country hope following the devastating natural disasters of the earthquake and tsunami that affected Japan that March.

The level of ticket sales, investment, commercial backing and TV and media coverage for the tournament was unprecedented. German crowds and travelling supporters packed stadiums throughout – 73,680 attended the opening match pitting Germany against Canada at Berlin's Olympiastadion, creating an incredible atmosphere.

But for some late-late goals and spot-kick dramas, the line-up in the final could actually have been very different.

Japan, who had lost 2–0 to England in group play, thwarted the German juggernaut in the quarter-finals with a solitary extra-time strike by Karina Maruyama. France owed their

Hosts Germany played out their opening game against Canada, a 2-1 win, at Berlin's Olympiastadion in front of a partisan and jubilant crowd of more than 70,000.

progress to the semi-finals to Elise Bussaglia's 88th-minute equalizer and some wayward England penalties in the shoot-out that followed.

Most astounding of all was USA versus Brazil, Abby Wambach's header, in time added on after extra time, levelling the score at 2–2. The Americans buried all five of their subsequent penalty kicks while Daiane missed hers. Marta's As Canarinhas headed home heartbroken.

After so much drama, the semi-finals were more straightforward, both games ending 3–1. Sweden's attacking flow against Japan was somewhat stunted without the injured Caroline Seger while the USA overpowered the flair of the French.

The final itself, however, was an epic. USA's all-out attacking pressure was matched by Japan's resistance, twice coming from behind, once in normal time and again through Sawa with three minutes remaining. Heartstopping moments included Azusa Iwashimizu's red card after 120 minutes, Ayumi Kaihori's shoot-out saves, and Saki Kumagai's winning kick.

It was a breathless and inspirational climax to a thrilling three weeks. Germany 2011 had taken the women's game to a whole new level.

Japan's talismanic captain Homare Sawa hoists the trophy to the skies after their courageous triumph against the USA in an epic encounter. A country had found a new set of heroines.

GROUP A

Germany	2	Canada	1
Nigeria	0	France	1
Germany	1	Nigeria	0
Canada	0	France	4
France	2	Germany	4
Canada	0	Nigeria	1

	P	W	D	L	F	A	Pts
Germany	3	3	0	0	7	3	9
France	3	2	1	2	7	4	6
Nigeria	3	1	0	2	1	2	3
Canada	3	0	0	3	1	7	0

GROUP B

Japan	2	New Zealand	1
Mexico	1	England	1
Japan	4	Mexico	0
New Zealand	1	England	2
England	2	Japan	0
New Zealand	2	Mexico	2

	P	W	D	L	F	A	Pts
England	3	2	1	0	5	2	7
Japan	3	2	0	1	6	3	6
Mexico	3	0	2	1	3	7	2
New Zealand	3	0	1	2	4	6	1

GROUP C

USA	2	Korea DPR	0
Colombia	0	Sweden	1
USA	3	Colombia	0
Korea DPR	0	Sweden	1
Sweden	2	USA	1
Korea DPR	0	Colombia	0

	P	W	D	L	F	A	Pts
Sweden	3	3	0	0	4	1	9
USA	3	2	0	1	6	2	6
Korea DPR	3	0	1	2	0	3	1
Colombia	3	0	1	2	0	4	1

GROUP D

Brazil	1	Australia	0
Norway	1	Eq. Guinea	0
Brazil	3	Norway	0
Australia	3	Eq. Guinea	2
Eq. Guinea	0	Brazil	3
Australia	2	Norway	1

	P	W	D	L	F	A	Pts
Brazil	3	3	0	0	7	0	9
Australia	3	2	0	1	5	4	6
Norway	3	1	0	2	2	5	3
Eq. Guinea	3	0	0	3	2	7	0

QUARTER-FINALS

Germany	0	Japan	1*
England	1 (3)	France	1 (4)*
Sweden	3	Australia	1
Brazil	2 (3)	USA	2 (5)*

*After extra time (on penalties)

SEMI-FINALS

Japan	3	Sweden	1
France	1	USA	3

THIRD-PLACE MATCH

Sweden	2	France	1

FINAL – 17 July: FIFA Women's World Cup Stadium, Frankfurt

Japan	2 (3)	USA	2 (1)*
Miyama (81)		Morgan (69)	*After extra time (on penalties)
Sawa (117)		Wambach (104)	
H-T: 0–0; F-T: 1–1		Att: 48,817	Ref: Steinhaus (Germany)

Japan: Kaihori, Kinga, Iwashimizu, Kumagai, Sakaguchi, Ando (Ogimi 66), Miyama, Kawasumi, Sawa, Ohno (Maruyama 66; Iwabuchi 119), Sameshima. **Sent off:** Iwashimizu (120+1)
USA: Solo, Rampone, Le Peilbet, Boxx, O'Reilly, Lloyd, Krieger, Holiday (Morgan 46), Rapinoe (Heath 114), Buehler, Wambach
Top scorers: 5 Sawa (Japan), 4 Marta (Brazil), 4 Wambach (USA)

FIFA WOMEN'S WORLD CUP QUIZ

Test your women's football knowledge. There are six different sections, with five teasers in each. How many can you get right? Answers can be found at the bottom of the page. Let's kick off…

FIRSTS

1. Which tournament top-scorer helped her team win the first FIFA Women's World Cup by netting twice in the final against Norway?

2. Who did China beat in the 1995 quarter-finals in the first-ever FIFA Women's World Cup match to go to penalties?

3. Who was the first female coach to win the FIFA Women's World Cup?

4. Who was the first (and so far only) player to be sent off in the final of a FIFA Women's World Cup?

5. Which team earned their first-ever FIFA Women's World Cup point when Hannah Wilkinson equalised in time added on against Mexico in 2011?

SECONDS

1. Which German was the second person to take a penalty in a FIFA Women's World Cup, and the first to score, in her team's 3–0 victory over Chinese Taipei?

2. Which Australian player set a FIFA Women's World Cup record for the quickest red card in the second minute of her country's final group game of 1999?

3. Who scored the second and final golden goal in FIFA Women's World Cup history to win the 2003 final?

4. Which former Sweden coach oversaw a second nation when she guided the hosts in 2007?

5. Who won the Golden Ball and Golden Shoe in 2007, as well as FIFA Women's World Player of the Year, despite only coming second in the FIFA Women's World Cup final?

GOAL-GETTERS

1. Which winning coach scored the 100th FIFA Women's World Cup goal, as a player, in 1995?

a) Silvia Neid
b) Norio Sasaki
c) Anson Dorrance

2. Which marvellous African superstar masterminded her team's first-ever victory in the FIFA Women's World Cup with a goal and an assist versus Korea DPR in 1999?

a) Perpetua Nkwocha
b) Mercy Akide
c) Genoveva Anonma

3. With 14 goals apiece, Marta and which other player are the highest-ever FIFA Women's World Cup goalscorers?

a) Birgit Prinz
b) Mia Hamm
c) Victoria Svensson

4. Who scored the latest goal in a game in FIFA Women's World Cup history to keep her team in their 2011 quarter-final?

a) Louisa Necib
b) Abby Wambach
c) Christine Sinclair

5. Who became the oldest player to score in a FIFA Women's World Cup final, at the age of 32 years and 314 days?

a) Heidi Store
b) Katia
c) Homare Sawa

TOUCH LINE

Can you unscramble the five head coaches and name their team, with just the year/years they were at the FIFA Women's World Cup as a hint?

1. Main Monster (2007, 2011)

2. Reclaim A Racoon (2011)

3. Corn And Reason (1991)

4. Pushed Again (2011)

5. Hollow Peep (2007, 2011)

CHAMPIONS!

1. Who went on to win the FIFA Women's World Cup twice after first appearing in a final on the losing side as a 17-year-old?

2. Which is the only team to have featured in the semi-finals of every FIFA Women's World Cup?

3. Which is the only nation to have won the FIFA Women's World Cup, the Women's Olympic Football Tournament and the UEFA European Women's Championship?

4. Who won the Golden Ball and the Golden Boot after leading her team to FIFA Women's World Cup glory in her fifth finals appearance?

5. Which two nations will be vying to win the FIFA Women's World Cup for a record third time in 2015?

MEMORABLE MOMENTS

1. Who is this unusual figure in goal against Denmark in 1995?

2. Who saved a penalty to help her team win the FIFA Women's World Cup in 1999?

3. Who celebrated her country's first FIFA Women's World Cup goals for 12 years in style?

4. Who spearheaded the shock of the tournament as the United States lost in the semi-finals in 2007?

5. Whose nose was broken in the opening match of the FIFA Women's World Cup 2011?

ANSWERS:
Firsts: 1. Michelle Akers of USA; 2. Sweden; 3. Tina Theune of Germany in 2003; 4. Azusa Iwashimizu of Japan; 5. New Zealand. **Seconds:** 1. Bettina Wiegmann; 2. Alicia Ferguson; 3. Nia Kunzer of Germany; 4. Marika Domanski Lyfors; 5.Marta of Brazil. **Goal-getters:** 1. a) Silvia Neid; 2. b) Mercy Akide; 3. a) Birgit Prinz; 4. b) Abby Wambach; 5. c) Homare Sawa. **On the Touch-Line:** 1. Tom Sermanni, Australia; 2. Carolina Morace, Canada; 3. Anson Dorrance, USA; 4. Pia Sundhage, USA; 5. Hope Powell, England. **Champions!:** 1. Birgit Prinz of Germany; 2. USA; 3. Norway; 4. Homare Sawa of Japan; 5. USA and Germany. **Memorable Moments:** 1. Mia Hamm of USA; 2. Briana Scurry of USA; 3. Kelly Smith of England; 4. Marta of Brazil. 5. Christine Sinclair of Canada.

KEY NOTES FOR THE MATCH SCHEDULE (PP16–17)

Notes for deciding the group stages

P = played (each team plays three group matches); W = win; D = draw; L = loss; F = goals scored (for); A = goals conceded (against); Pts = points. Three points for a win; one for a draw; no points for a loss.

After most points, groups are decided first by better positive goal difference, then total goals scored. After this, the head-to-head results will decide the order, and if three teams are involved, it is again goal difference in these matches, then goals scored. If teams are still equal, then the FIFA Organising Committee will draw lots.

Explanation of knock-out stages

All knock-out matches will be decided on the day. If the scores are level after 90 minutes, extra time (two 15-minute periods) will be played. If the scores remain level, kicks from the penalty mark (penalty shoot-out) will decide the winner. Teams will take five kicks, alternately, unless one team cannot win after three or four attempts. If the scores are still level after 10 attempts, then a sudden-death shoot-out follows, decided by one team scoring and the other failing.

The alpha-numeric designations in the second round refer to first-round group positions. 1A is the winner of Group A, 2F is the runner-up in Group F. The four third-placed teams with the best records in the first round will join the group winners and runners-up. The third-placed teams will play the winner of a group other than the one in which they have already played.

The match numbers are the official tournament match numbers and W before the number refers to the winners of that tie (L denotes losers), thus the first semi-final, match 49, will be between the winners of quarter-final matches 45 and 46.

AUTHORS' ACKNOWLEDGEMENTS

Compiling this book would not have been possible without the assistance of the following generous people and supporters of the women's game, so we offer our gratitude to: Kevin Ashby, Jennifer Ast, Cintia Barlem, David Barber, Sven Beyrich, Peter Davis, Nicola Demaine, Tony DiCicco, Moya Dodd, Carolina Garcia, Scott Gleba, Paul Green, Aaron Heifetz, Markus Helbling, Fran Hilton-Smith, Jeremy Ruane, Paul Saffer, Ruth Scheithauer, Dawn Scott, Richard Scott, Alex Stone, Julie Teo and Steven Upfold. We would also particularly like to thank the following association and confederation websites for quotes used: fifa.com, the-afc.com, canadasoccer.com, concacaf.com, conmebol.com, uefa.com.

CREDITS

The publishers would like to thank the following sources for their kind permission to reproduce the pictures in this book.

A young Canada fan cheers on her team at the FIFA U-20 Women's World Cup Canada 2014. Now her nation will welcome the best in the world in the senior women's game.